T0268909

The
Episcopal
Way

VOLUME 1
in the
Church's
Teachings
for a
Changing
World
series

ERIC H. F. LAW AND STEPHANIE SPELLERS

Morehouse Publishing
NEW YORK · HARRISBURG · DENVER

Unless otherwise noted, the Scripture quotations contained herein are from the New Revised Standard Version Bible, copyright © 1989 by the Division of Christian Education of the National Council of Churches of Christ in the U.S.A. Used by permission. All rights reserved.

Morehouse Publishing, 4785 Linglestown Road, Suite 101,
    Harrisburg, PA 17112
Morehouse Publishing, 19 East 34th Street, New York, NY 10016
Morehouse Publishing is an imprint of Church Publishing Incorporated.
www.churchpublishing.org

Cover art: "The Last Supper" by Olukayode Babalola
Cover design by Laurie Klein Westhafer
Interior design and typesetting by Beth Oberholtzer

Library of Congress Cataloging-in-Publication Data

Law, Eric H. F.
    The Episcopal way / Eric H.F. Law and Stephanie Spellers.
        pages cm.—(The church's teachings for a changing world series ; Volume 1)
    Includes bibliographical references.
    ISBN 978-0-8192-2960-1 (pbk.)—ISBN 978-0-8192-2961-8 (ebook)
1. Episcopal Church—Doctrines. 2. Episcopal Church—Customs and practices. 3. Christianity and culture—United States. I. Title.
    BX5930.3.L39 2014
    283'.73--dc23

                                                            2014013229

Printed in the United States of America

Contents

Preface to the Series

Since 1949, Episcopal Church leaders have turned to the Church's Teaching series for help discovering the heart of the Episcopal Way. Together, the books provided a weighty yet timely overview of Episcopal identity, practice, and tradition: our history, worship, theology, ethics, and our approach to scripture, contemporary society, and the practice of ministry. One topic, one book, at a time.

For generations, these have been key titles on clergy bookshelves. Updated in the late 1970s and again at the close of the 1990s, they captured the essential body of knowledge for Episcopalians. The books have increasingly aimed to speak to wider audiences, to be at home in the seminary or in the church library, content-rich enough for clergy but accessible enough for non-seminary trained laypeople.

Today—halfway through the second decade of the twenty-first century, nearly twenty years after the last series was launched—the very ground we walk on has shifted. September 11th. The Internet and social media. Globalism. The decline of mainline churches. The rise of secularism. Across the Episcopal Church, people have asked for new teaching resources that bring generations of wisdom to meet a rapidly changing world.

At the Episcopal Church's General Convention in 2012, Eric H. F. Law and Stephanie Spellers, together with Church Publishing's Editorial Director Nancy Bryan, sat together and began crafting the shape for a new series. As the editors, Eric and Stephanie—both of us priests, authors, teachers, and curriculum developers—were familiar with and grateful for the series' previous incarnations. As people of color who are younger than the average Episcopalian (as of 2012: 62), we had ourselves yearned for resources that would place the teachings of the Episcopal Church in the context of ministry in an evolving world rich with difference—new contexts, new power dynamics, new technologies, and new and shifting values.

While some churches can ignore and even resist change in the surrounding culture, the Episcopal Church is not one of them. Our traditions, teachings, and practices always weave the catholic (which means it is part of a universal church, one that spans culture, time, region, and perspective) together with the particular and contextual. The Episcopal Way is flexible enough and generous enough to bridge an ancient faith with new contexts.

All of which brings us to this moment, and this new series, "Church's Teachings for a Changing World."

A New Series for a New Moment

Like the Church's Teaching series of the past, this one seeks to engage Episcopal newcomers, members, and leaders in faithful, thoughtful conversations about how this particular branch of Christianity approaches God and embodies Jesus Christ. We hope you learn more about the Episcopal Church and the Episcopal Way. We hope you fall (more) deeply in love with it. We also hope you find here language *and* practices that equip you to share the church's teachings, not just as rote history but as a captivating and life-giving story.

How will we accomplish that? The series will feature nine books, including the introductory book you now hold and a summary book to wrap the series and point the way forward. In between, seven books will cover seven topics:

- **Scripture:** Understanding how the Bible—including the Hebrew Scriptures (the Old Testament) and the Christian Scriptures (the New Testament)—reveals God's love and God's will for individuals and communities. The big question: How do Episcopalians read the Bible?

- **Church History:** The story of the Episcopal Church and the Christian story of which it is a part (from the first centuries after Jesus, through the birth of the Church of England in the sixteenth century, and especially the main American expression of Anglicanism, the Episcopal Church). The driving question: How did this church even come into being?

- **Theology:** Literally "God-talk"—theo (God) + logos (talk)—theology is the result of people of faith in every era answering the question: What's God got to do with it?

- **Ethics:** In the Episcopal Way, we take into account the Bible, our traditions, and our God-given power to reason in order to make difficult decisions. The driving question: How do Episcopalians decide the right thing to do?

- **Contemporary Society:** The various political and social issues that concern people of faith and people with no particular faith: the environment, technology, racism, economic inequality, human sexuality, and so forth. In other words: How do Episcopalians reckon with life in a changing world?

- **Worship:** Also known as liturgy, that is, "the work of the people," or the various ways that we pray, sing, teach, and make offering to God as Christians. The driving question here would be: How do Episcopalians pray?

- **Practice of Ministry:** All the ways to share the good news of God's love, grace, and justice as individuals and in community. The question: How do Episcopalians do God's work within the church and beyond?

The seven topics will sound familiar to anyone who has studied in an Episcopal seminary, because they are the seven "canonical areas" around which most schools arrange their studies. They should also make some intuitive sense. If you were drawing a picture of the church as a body, these topics would encompass the church's life from head to heart to toe, internal organs to bones to skin.

Each topic—each book—will be treated by an author who brings multiple and varied gifts to the project: they are scholars and experts in the area, and they are active practitioners deeply rooted in the changing landscape where we now live out our faith. These authors have accepted a hefty mission:

- **Acknowledge and embrace new paradigms.** Help us to think, pray, and act in a multi-cultural, tech-savvy, networked, global landscape. If those words sound like jargon of a different sort, hang tight; you will see more on these points in the pages that follow.

- **Offer content and processes geared to changing contexts.** In other words, don't just share the information, but show us how it's done—in one-on-one conversation, in a class, via social media, via art, and through other modes entirely.

- **Say it plain, please.** Authors are strongly encouraged to practice the first Road Rule: beware of "Episco-speak," the insider language and jargon that any community develops, which serves as shorthand for members and a stumbling block for people who are not already in the group. When jargon comes up, we'll try to make it plain and user friendly—in twenty-five words or less.

- **Invite us into open dialogue.** Instead of insiders talking to other insiders, imagine people in conversation with neighbors and strangers about the depth of Episcopal and Christian teaching and life. Frame chapters with good questions, so we get skilled at addressing real questions with real people, and not simply talking one church-nerd to another.

- **Keep it interactive, not static.** Each book features chapters written in digestible lengths (five to eight pages) and in a style that stands between textbook and blog entry.

- **Take it home.** Most chapters also include an activity readers can engage either as part of a community or online. For example:

> **TRY THIS** Now go online and look up the words *mission, missionary, missional*. What's out there?

You'll also find "Road Rules" throughout the books. They boxes feature tips for engaging in actual conversation and interaction in the world. For example:

> **Road Rule 1** Be careful using church jargon. If you can't explain it in 25 words of fairly standard language, then find another word.

- **Grow a multi-media learning community.** Each book is hooked to a whole web of conversation and resources which you will find at www.churchpublishing.org/episcopalway. We expect that small groups and classes will use the accompanying online study guides. We encourage groups to head to web communities for each book, where they can post their own stories, questions, tips, and new content. Who knows? The next generation's series may be born from those pages.

PART I

Introduction

Chapter 1

Discovering the Episcopal Way

Imagine the scene: A long-time Episcopalian and a college student are working beside each other at the local soup kitchen:

Mark: What's an Episcopalian?

Susan: How did you know I'm an Episcopalian?

Mark: Your apron. It says, "Hug me, I'm an Episcopalian."

Susan: Oh. Yes, I go to St. Paul's Church, just down the street. We've been on the same corner for 150 years and just completed a million-dollar renovation of our organ.

Mark: I think I know the building you're talking about. It has red doors. I thought it might be closed, but if you're there Sunday mornings, I guess that's why I never saw the doors open. So tell me again: what's an Episcopalian?

Susan: Well, we're a liturgical church, maintaining catholic traditions, but we're not the Roman Catholic Church. We're part of the Anglican Communion, a whole family of churches that stem from the Church of England. The Episcopal Church is the branch rooted here in America, founded just as the Revolutionary War finished.

Mark: (silence) No offense, but I'm not sure what a lot of what you said means. Liturgical? catholic but not Catholic? Anglican?

Susan: Maybe you heard about us on the news several years ago? The gay bishop?

Mark: Right! You're the ones who split over homosexuality.

Susan: We didn't actually split. Some folks did leave, but Episcopalians describe ourselves as following the Via Media, and that means we can hold many theological perspectives in tension, but still gather at the same Eucharistic table.

Mark: (silence)

Susan: Did I lose you again?

Mark: It's okay. How about we get started? I think the guests are coming in now.

Susan is not the only one who struggles to explain her church's story. Many Episcopalians can recall that moment in the soup kitchen, or on the train, or at the dinner table, when the questions arose . . .

"What's an Episcopalian, anyway?"

"What is the Church of England?"

"How do you read the Bible?"

"Is your church doing anything around justice?"

There are good answers to those questions, but the words—and the content—may not come when we need them most. No matter how genuine our desire to connect and welcome others, many church members struggle to find the information or a way to share it in the real world. It is one thing to tell what the Episcopal Church is *not,* but naming what it *is* seems strangely difficult.

It's not just a struggle for laypeople. Clergy are well trained for academic discourse about historical-critical scriptural interpretation, soteriology, and postmodern missional engagement. But the teachings aren't worth much if you don't know how to talk faith in everyday language with the woman next to you on the bus, the people behind you in line for movie tickets, the maintenance man who sees a cross in your living room, or the friend in the hospital who doesn't understand why God would let this happen to her.

Road Rule 2 Practice Holy Curiosity: In the midst of a conversation, listen with curiosity and pay attention to the other person's story, experience, values, belief, struggles, passion, pain, joy, etc. When it is time for you to share your own story, you will be better prepared to truly connect with your conversation partner.

Back in the 1950s, it was a safe assumption that people in the United States went to church and had a working knowledge of Christianity. On the flip side, if a family did not go to church on Sunday—perhaps they were followers of a different religion or had no religion at all—they might earn suspicious looks from the neighbors. Churches thrived under this favoritism. The presumption was: If we have a better building, a better music program, a better youth group—if we do what we do better—people will choose us.

The whole system depended on a cultural norm that favored the church. That norm is gone.

The Church/World Rift

There is a lot more to this story and this struggle, and we will explore it soon. For now, it is enough to note that, in the absence of this cultural norm, a new landscape has emerged. To begin, there are the "emerging" or "emergent" generations (such as the young person in our opening dialogue). For Christians in this group, going to church on Sunday is one of several options, and not the most popular. In fact, a growing proportion of people born after 1965 (Generations X and Y and the Millennials) now claim no faith at all—32 percent of people ages 18–29 and 21 percent of people 30–49.[1] Much of their knowledge of Christians, Christianity, and the church today comes from the media or outdated stories from their childhood. Many church people do not know how to

---

1. http://www.pewforum.org/2012/10/09/nones-on-the-rise/#who-are-the-unaffiliated

speak to this younger generation. As a result, emerging generations increasingly don't connect to faith communities at all.

A similar chasm separates churches from a growing proportion
of the American population. Diana Butler Bass talks about this
turn-of-the-century shift in *Christianity After Religion: The End
of Church and the Beginning of a New Spiritual Awakening:*

> The first years of the twenty-first century marked a swift and
> shocking reversal of the religious mood of the late 1990s. Before
> the millennium, American religion went through a period of opti-
> mism, growth, and wealth. Indeed, from 1990 to 2000, Americans
> expressed increasing confidence in religious institutions and reli-
> gious leaders. The religious favorable rating now hovers around
> the confidence rank of Wall Street and major corporations.[2]

Why the sinking sentiment? People look around and see the
troubles of the post-9/11 world and can't help but blame religion for being part of the problem instead of the solution. Sex
abuse and embezzlement, battles over sexuality, withdrawal from
wounded neighborhoods, religious wars, rituals and doctrines that
appear other-worldly and disconnected from daily life—each has
played its part in driving a wedge between people in the church
and the communities around us.

Show Me the Way

If church is no longer privileged, then Christians will need to become missional, that is, outwardly focused on relationship with
people who are not part of church, and even with people who are in
church but stand at the margins, so that together we can share the
life and love of Jesus. If Episcopalians are going to get missional and build meaningful relationships with people around us, we

---

2. Diana Butler Bass, *Christianity After Religion: The End of Church and the
Birth of a New Spiritual Awakening* (New York: HarperCollins, 2012), 81–82.

must do two things: 1) be curious and open to other cultures and perspectives, and 2) be mature in our understanding of our Christian and Episcopal identity.

missional: heading out to share and discover God's love, in relationship with people who are not part of church

The first part—being curious and receptive—happens as we get to know the stories of people who are not part of church. It happens when we cross boundaries and open to embrace the Other (the one who is different from the "norm," who is not part of the church, or who holds less power in the church).

The second move is just as important: church folks will need to spend time getting to know and share the things that give shape and life to our Christian identity. For Episcopalians, that means a better understanding of something called the Episcopal Way: not simply a common set of doctrines, ideas, or even words to pray, but a combination of practices, attitudes, and an approach to God known as a "Way."

There are plenty of reasons to appreciate this phrase, The Episcopal Way. First, because the early disciples were known as followers of "the Way," before they were even called Christians (see Acts 9:2). Jesus called himself "the *way*, the truth and the life," and those who turned their lives inside out to identify with him were knowingly following the Way.

Second, speaking of the Way, as in a path or road, suggests that the Episcopal Way is a journey. Indeed, it begins with the original story of Jesus' disciples and winds through centuries of the church's development, failure, and redemption. It continues to this day, as we face an exhilarating and quickly changing world. It broadens into a future for which we must remain flexible, curious, and grounded. Walk even a little while with Episcopalians, and you understand that for us faith is a journey, one with a beginning, a middle, but no true end . . . except closer relationship with God through Jesus Christ.

The Episcopal Way: the combination of practices, attitudes, and approaches to God nurtured by the Episcopal Church

Finally, a "way" is a method, style, or manner of doing something. For us, this means the Episcopal Way is not just something you believe; it is something you do. A Latin phrase captures this wisdom: *lex orandi, lex credendi.* Loosely translated, it means: "the law of praying is the law of believing." In other words, the way we pray shapes or conditions the way we believe. You become Episcopalian by practicing the Episcopal method of following Jesus, praying as Episcopalians have prayed for centuries, and living the Episcopal style of building community and relating to neighbors. No signature on a faith statement is required. Live with us, pray with us, practice the Way with us, weave it into your own life. Then you will understand. It is a roomy way of being Christian, and a deeply faithful one.

No wonder it was hard for Susan, the long-time Episcopalian in the conversation at the beginning of the chapter, to explain the Episcopal Church to Mark, the young adult at the soup kitchen. The Episcopal Way can be tough to summarize in twenty-five words or less, especially in a world with an increasingly short attention span, instant access to information, and a penchant for multi-tasking. Yet, this way of being Christian might just be an ideal fit for the communities where we live and move today.

The Episcopal Way brings the stories and eternal truth of scripture alive so that we hear God's voice speaking in our everyday lives. This Way challenges each generation to learn and appreciate tradition, and to add its own wisdom to the constant process of updating and translating traditions so they continue to speak today. This Way celebrates the gift of reason, so we can engage the world as it is and figure out the path that leads us closest to God's dream.

As Episcopalians, we don't claim to be perfect at following the Way, and God knows we have made our share of mistakes on the journey. Yet even these imperfections have their place—they remind us that it is not our power, but the grace and love of God that carry us through this sometimes messy, often confusing, always shifting process of fully living as Jesus' body in the world.

What, then, is the way forward? In this pluralistic world, there is simply no way to be all things to all people. There is also no way to attempt to remain unchanged and protect ourselves from the cultural shifts all around. We believe the journey starts with learning and loving our authentic story, the Episcopal Way. The more we know ourselves—our values, our patterns, our myths—the more secure we will feel and the more we can explore changing contexts without the fear of losing ourselves. Grounded like that, we can move into our wider communities, listening and sharing and even rejoicing when the Episcopal Way takes on forms we never imagined. If we are proud of our tradition and secure in God's love, we can be generous, honest, and fearless, walking with Jesus into new places and new relationships.

That balanced perspective plays out in the actual shape of this book. **Part II: The Church Meets a Changing World** examines some of the paradigm shifts that mark life in the second decade of the twenty-first century. For each shift, we look to a unique element of the Episcopal Way and explore what this church could teach and share to offer life and hope in a world changing faster than most of us can track.

Part III: The World Meets a Changing Church shifts the focus and takes a loving but honest look at Episcopal Church life, especially considering how we have fallen short of the promise of the Way. This section listens for the wisdom of the communities around us, because we trust that the world has a lot to teach the

Here is our simple summary of the Way. Try it on or go to www.churchpublishing.org/episcopalway to make your own comments:

What's an Episcopalian? We follow Jesus with our souls, minds, and arms open wide, ready to love God, our neighbors, and the world.

Jesus Christ was (and is) both/and, drawing together human *and* divine. We hope to be both/and Christians, drawing together and embracing ancient traditions *and* the wisdom just over the horizon, reason *and* mystery, beauty *and* justice, catholic *and* Protestant, discipline *and* freedom, body *and* Spirit, deep faith *and* probing questions, the cross *and* the resurrection.

This is The Episcopal Way of following Jesus. Let's walk.

church. We need that wisdom and those partners—and we need to be ready to change—if we are going to be true to the beautiful path that is the Episcopal Way of following Jesus.

TRY THIS If you're part of an Episcopal Church, try to complete the following sentences:

Being an Episcopalian is . . .

Being an Episcopalian is not . . .

Belonging to the Episcopal Church is . . .

Belonging to the Episcopal Church is not . . .

There are, however, two conditions in completing this exercise:

1. Use everyday language, with no church jargon except the word "Jesus."
2. No sentence can be longer than 140 characters.

What part of this exercise did you find easy? What did you find difficult? Why? Go to www.churchpublishing.org/episcopalway and read what others have shared and add your comments.

Chapter 2

What's the Story?

If you're going to trace the Episcopal Way, you've got to begin with the earliest followers of Jesus. Eventually, you come to England, where Christians flourished for a thousand years as an extension of the Holy Roman Catholic Church.

The Way took a sharp turn in 1534, after King Henry VIII made his politically (and romantically) motivated break from the Pope. While the move coincided with the Reformation—a movement that brought freedom from Roman Catholic control and greater emphasis on scripture and local languages—Henry wasn't exactly a reformer. He had no great desire to depart from Catholic practices and doctrines; he just wanted to separate them from Rome's control. The English Church was still the Catholic Church in England.

Under Henry's son King Edward VI, the Reformation finally took root in England. Archbishop of Canterbury Thomas Cranmer, architect of the first Book of Common Prayer (1549), received greater latitude under Edward and used it to edge England further on the road to change.

Queen Mary stepped to the throne in 1553 and cut the reform movement short. As Protestants clashed with Roman sympathizers, churches were burned, and royals and church leaders (including Cranmer himself) were killed. Finally, in 1559, Queen Elizabeth took power and demanded a compromise to bring the two groups together in one church under one governor: the Queen. That compromise was the Elizabethan Settlement.

Introducing the Via Media

The Elizabethan Settlement established the attitude that most defines the heart of Anglicanism: the Via Media. Literally "The Middle Way," this way struggles to find a holy "both/and" course between two or more options, rather than an exclusive either/or, winner/loser path.

Early on, the still-new Church of England carved a middle way that would be at once catholic and Protestant. Under Elizabeth, there were still priests and bishops, and they wore simple, catholic vestments. However, Anglican clergy did not pledge allegiance to the Pope or pray in Latin, and they placed a prayer book full of scriptures in the hands of the people—a decidedly Protestant turn.

The Via Media does more than carve a path between catholic and Protestant traditions. It also gives us that most Anglican piece of furniture: the three-legged stool—a balanced approach that appeals to the authority of Scripture, Tradition, and Reason. Picture the three components balanced like this:

Scripture: *the record of the original revelations of God's relationship with humanity especially through the ancient Israelites and Jesus.* From the outset, we acknowledge that the scriptures are the word of God and contain everything necessary for salvation (the statement shows up in all the Episcopal ordination services and in several of our historic documents). We focus on the scriptures as the principle authority for how we live, and how we understand and seek the will of God.

Tradition: *the continuing revelation of God through the guidance of the Holy Spirit.* We turn to traditions—the prayers, doctrines, practices, structures, and stories developed over time as a source for authority. They are rooted in scripture, but they also emerge as communities listen for the still-lively presence of Christ in their midst over the ages.

Via Media: "The Middle Way" or a comprehensive, "both/and" path that draws on the wisdom of multiple perspectives

The church, as a worshiping body of faithful people, has for two thousand years amassed experience of God, and what they have said to us through the centuries is critical for interpreting scripture and interpreting the world.

Reason: *thoughtful engagement with the present reality, both local and global.* Episcopalians believe God has given us intelligence and our own experience. Holding the biblical text, knowing what Christians have taught through the ages, we still have to arrive at the truth in relation to our own lives and times.

Scriptures, Tradition, and Reason: they rely on each other, lean on each other, and create a solid foundation for faith. Given the chance to cling to one source and ignore the others, the Episcopal Way forces us to do the hard work of holding them together.

The writers of the Preface to the 1662 Book of Common Prayer knew that balanced approach was crucial for a developing faith community. They lifted the virtue of "keep[ing] the mean between the two extremes, of too much stiffness in refusing, and of too much easiness in admitting any variation from it."[3]

The same words show up in the Book of Common Prayer here in America. On the one hand, they remind us not to go running after every trend; on the other hand, they help us to receive new input with curiosity and grace. Pause, consider the complex realities around you, and then figure out where, in the space between, the truth may be found. It is the Episcopal Way.

---

3. Preface to the 1662 Book of Common Prayer, inspired by Aristotle.

The Heart of Anglicanism

That Via Media impulse colors the Episcopal Church and the entire Anglican Communion to this day. In their collection *Beyond Colonial Anglicanism: The Anglican Communion in the Twenty-first Century*, Episcopal scholars Kwok Pui Lan and Ian Douglas offer two definitions of Anglican identity, both grounded in the Via Media. Douglas says it this way:

> The advent of the Church of England marked a reconception of the body of Christ on the English shores that was at once profoundly particular and profoundly catholic. This process of contextualization, in which the church becomes grounded in the local realities of a particular people while remaining in communion across the differences of culture and geography . . . is where Anglican identity lies. Anglicanism thus can be understood as the embrace and celebration of apostolic catholicity within vernacular moments.[4]

In other words, Anglican Christians honor and celebrate the traditions passed from the earliest centuries of Christianity (what Douglas means by "apostolic catholicity"). But that celebration has to occur in "vernacular moments": the place, time, culture, and context within which we find ourselves at this moment. This ground, this life, this changing world—this is where we translate the message of Jesus and make it real among real people. If the translation does not happen, if the catholic traditions are not translated into the language and culture of real people, then it isn't yet Anglican.

Kwok Pui Lan could not agree more. As she explains:

> Anglicanism was a cultural hybrid from the beginning . . . As a cultural hybrid of Catholicism and Protestantism, the Church of England in the sixteenth century assimilated elements from both traditions to create a very fluid identity.[5]

---

4. Ian Douglas and Kwok Pui Lan, eds., *Beyond Global Anglicanism: The Anglican Communion in the 21st Century* (New York: Church Publishing, 2001), 35.
5. Ibid., 56.

Fluidity and hybridity: you often hear the words used to describe today's world. They also describe the Episcopal Way. This is a fluid, hybrid church, deeply connected to local cultures and deeply connected with ancient traditions. A church rooted in the Via Media.

Anglican Communion: the global family of churches that share roots in the Church of England and express Anglican tradition in relation to their unique, local contexts

Today, we have another opportunity to walk the Via Media. Imagine if we could know, live, and love our traditions, all the while finding ways to adapt them to share the good news of Jesus Christ in a changing world. That is our task in this book and in this series.

Road Rule 3 Beware of simplistic conclusions like either/or, right/wrong, good/bad, sinner/saint, especially in matters of faith. The Episcopal Way considers widely differing, even contradictory ideas before coming to resolution.

Why Do We Care?

We've now highlighted essential parts of the Anglican and Episcopal story. It is only right that we share our own stories and explain why we care about this Episcopal Way and how it is lived, taught, and shared for generations to come.

Eric is a third-generation Christian and a second-generation Anglican, born into a family linked to the Anglican missionary ministry in China and Hong Kong. Although he is a cradle Episcopalian, Eric was not able to fully claim his faith until his family immigrated to the United States in 1970 and joined an Episcopal church in New York's Chinatown. Later he attended Cornell University and took part in the Episcopal campus ministry. Eventually, at Episcopal Divinity School, he discovered words and concepts like Via Media and claimed even more of the Episcopal tradition as his own.

In 1984, as the Episcopal campus minister at the University of Southern California, he worked with students and helped them to understand and share their faith as Christians and Episcopalians in diverse contexts. That led him to write his first book, *The Wolf Shall Dwell with the Lamb,* intended to help leaders to function and claim faith in diverse multi-cultural contexts.

In 1996, Eric accepted the call to be the Ministry and Congregational Development Officer of the Anglican Diocese of New Westminster in British Columbia, Canada. He worked intensively with more than fifty congregations seeking to respond to an already changed world while being authentically Anglican. During this time, he wrote his third book, *Inclusion: Making Room for Grace,* which described theologically and practically how to be an inclusive community in a diverse and changing world. In 2001, he took over as Missioner for Congregational Development for the Episcopal Diocese of Los Angeles, where he worked with more than sixty congregations fostering transformational change. During this time, he focused on teaching and preaching in multi-contextual communities and wrote *The Word at the Crossing.* In other words, through his responses to the needs of local church communities, he taught and wrote about the Via Media.

In 2006, he founded the Kaleidoscope Institute, which equips churches to be missional, multi-cultural, and sustainable. His latest project, *Holy Currencies,* teaches local church leaders to connect with people in their communities through the creation of sustainable, missional ministries.

Raised in the South in a black, loosely Baptist family, Stephanie took a winding road into the Episcopal Church. At Wake Forest University in North Carolina, she studied Eastern religions and meditated; she also sang in a gospel choir and got excited about liberation theology (Christianity from the perspective of oppressed groups). In 1996, she entered Harvard Divinity School, planning to get a doctorate in Buddhism, but quickly steered aside to study American religious history, especially the role of religion in movements for social change. She took that background to work as a religion reporter for a newspaper in Tennessee. Eventually, telling other people's religious stories sparked her desire for a faith of her own.

Stephanie moved back to Cambridge to work at Harvard Divinity School and dove into church. She was baptized in 1998 at a multi-cultural, politically active, largely low-income Lutheran church in Roxbury, Massachusetts, but something was still missing. She needed incarnation: a God who joins us in flesh and embraces and transforms every part of creation. She needed action: partnering with God to make God's dream reality. She needed beauty: seeing feelings and awe as part of how we meet God. She found all that and more in the Episcopal Church. Then she got passionate about sharing this historic, vibrant Episcopal Way *and* seeing Anglicanism embraced and adapted by groups on the margins.

Stephanie launched the Radical Welcome project in 2003, traveling the country to study and interview hundreds of Episcopalians working to embrace their margins; the fruit of that journey is the book, *Radical Welcome: Embracing God, the Other, and the Spirit of Transformation* (2006). Concurrent with that research, she completed a second master's degree at Episcopal Divinity School in 2004 and was ordained an Episcopal priest in 2005. She immediately began forming The Crossing, a worship community based at St. Paul's Episcopal Cathedral in Boston. A true hybrid of emerging cultures and Anglican traditions, The Crossing broke new ground and continues to nurture and inspire leaders near and far.

In 2012, Stephanie moved to Brooklyn, New York, to serve as Canon for Missional Vitality in the Diocese of Long Island, a large and diverse diocese that embraces all of Brooklyn, Queens, and Long Island. The co-author of *Ancient Faith, Future Mission: Fresh Expressions in the Sacramental Traditions* (with Ian Mobsby and Graham Cray), she has written many more articles and

God's mission: what God is up to in the world—restoring all people to unity and wholeness with God and each other

book chapters and edited numerous books on missional church for Church Publishing. The chaplain to the Episcopal House of Bishops, she has also served as the co-chair of the Episcopal Church's Standing Commission on Mission and Evangelism, and regularly speaks, writes, and creates curricula designed to help the Episcopal Church to engage in passionate mission with a changing world.

• • •

We both have deep love and fervent dreams for the Episcopal Church and its calling in the world. We've both had moments where we saw the church living for God's mission (or what God is up to in the world: the Episcopal Church says God welcomes us to join in the restoration project, bringing everyone back into unity with God and with each other[6]). We have seen the church shining brightly and joining others to heal and love our broken yet beautiful neighborhoods and world. We want to see that happen even more.

Everything we offer in these pages comes as a prayer that God's dream would be known and made real, in the church we love, in the leaders and members with whom we walk, and in countless neighbors and strangers who might share God's dream, too.

TRY THIS Write or share the story of your spiritual experience. If you are an Episcopalian, incorporate your understanding of the Episcopal Way. If you are new to the church, write about your experience of the presence of God, the higher power, the divine, or holiness as an individual and in relationship with others. Share your writing with a friend or with a group.

---

6. "An Outline of the Faith," Book of Common Prayer (New York: Church Publishing, 1979), 855.

PART II

The Church Meets a Changing World

Early in the Hebrew Bible, in the book of Deuteronomy, the tribes of Israel were exiled from their homes into the wilderness. For forty years Moses led the ragged band on their rough passage, wandering and struggling, seeking the land God promised to give them. On the eve of their entry into the land of Canaan, waiting on the plains of Moab, Moses stepped forward to share a message: The world you are about to enter will challenge and tempt you. Do not forget the commandments and teachings God has given you.

He concluded with a sharp reminder that echoes through the ages, "I call heaven and earth to witness against you today that I have set before you life and death, blessings and curses. Choose life so that you and your descendants may live" (Deuteronomy 30:19).

The America we now inhabit is every bit wilderness, moving faster, filled with emerging voices and cultures, playing out in the flesh and online, the local going global and the global suddenly at the front door. This world, like the land of Canaan, is equally rife

19

with blessings and curses. The Episcopal Way assumes God will use the very stuff of life around us to bless and teach us . . . if we choose life.

In the chapters that follow, we lay out some of the tectonic shifts that have changed America in just the last fifteen to twenty-five years: the digital revolution, patterns of brain functioning, networking theory, flattened authority, globalism, and secularization. Most of these developments did not start and end in this short period, but each has expanded (or our consciousness of it has shifted) in such a way that life today is simply not the same as it was at even the turn of the century.

For each shift, we will name its related blessing as well as the potential shadow or "curse." We will then identify and explore some core element of the Episcopal Way that could meet this new world reality: incarnation, liturgy, networks, democracy, the vernacular, and reason balanced with mystery.

Some might wonder if we are trying to make the Episcopal Church "relevant." We are much more concerned here with digging deep to discover how this church's traditions, teachings, and practices speak to, participate in, *and* challenge the culture within which we live out the good news. We want to know, as the Israelites wondered (and as every faith community must discern), how to choose blessing and life. And we want to help our neighbors and our world to do the same.

Here is how the chapters will unfold:

Changing World	The Episcopal Way
Internet and social media: Life is high tech but low touch; social media is becoming a primary forum for interaction.	**Incarnation:** God dwells in the world in flesh and blood, and in sacraments, affirming our bodies and face-to-face interaction.
Brain functioning: Our brain wiring seems to be changing, thanks to multi-tasking, flashing images, and the digital flood of information.	**Liturgy:** We gather for a multi-sensory experience rooted in consistent, ancient rhythms that anchor our wandering bodies and souls.
Networking and emergent theory: Connections and networks determine what we know and who we are, sometimes with severe limitations and barriers.	**Networks:** Church is organized into circles and networks, from the local to the international, and links us with past, present, and future.
Flattened authority: Liberation movements and collaborative models have reduced our tolerance for top-down leadership.	**Democracy:** Laypeople exercise authority alongside clergy, all within vertical structures that balance and organize our shared work.
Globalization: Cultural boundaries rub closer than ever, hybrids crop up everywhere, but local traditions can fade away.	**Indigenous:** The gospel and traditions get translated into the language and culture of the people on the ground.
Secularism: A growing number of us claim no religion at all, leaving church sitting on the margins.	**Reason and mystery:** Reason allows us to engage and dialogue with a changing world, even as mystery sets us free from needing all the answers.

Chapter 3

Digital Media and the Incarnation

Technologies have always functioned as an extension of our bodies. A hammer, a knife, a rope—all help to amplify what our hands intend but cannot otherwise accomplish. The same is true for digital technologies: the telephone is an extension of the ears and mouth. Without a telephone, you can only hear and speak to someone within a limited distance; with this device, you can have intimate conversation with someone on the other side of the earth.

Likewise, the computer and the Internet function as extensions of our brain. In the last fifteen years, tech experts have created means to manage generations of data in devices that cost a little more than a few hardcover books. Why try to recall the signers of the Declaration of Independence when you can Google it?

This means the so-called digital natives—those who were born after 1995—are the most extended and powerfully connected generation the human community has ever known. The digital natives easily access information, make friends, and create communities within an expansive digital world. They make it look like child's play.

Most older generations—the digital aliens—are not natives of this landscape, but we have adapted to digital reality with varying degrees of proficiency and comfort. We bypass a trip to the mall or Main Street because we can shop on the Internet and have the goods delivered to our front door, sometimes within twenty-four hours. Who needs to set foot in a bank when our handheld devices allow us to make financial transactions in bed, at work, or on the beach? We can share words, music, stories, and images with hundreds or thousands of friends simultaneously, anywhere, anytime.

The Internet has eliminated the distances that once slowed the exchange of information. It also connects us in real time. For previously isolated individuals or communities, digital social media is, indeed, a blessing that links them to resources and communities. For example, Eric's mother was hospitalized for a long period of time, and he was alone at the hospital with her. Through social media, he connected with friends around the world, who prayed and provided him with much-needed encouragement and support. Thanks to the Internet, he was not alone.

The Shadow: So Near Yet So Far

The Internet may also help to create distance and block intimacy at the local level. Peter Block is an organizational consultant and proponent of healthy communities. He has noticed a dramatic loss of genuine human connection in the face of the digital revolution:

> The absence of belonging is so widespread that we might say we are living in an age of isolation. . . . Ironically, we talk today of how small our world has become, with the shrinking effect of globalization, instant sharing of information, quick technologies, workplaces that operate around the globe. Yet these do not necessarily create a sense of belonging. They provide connection, diverse information, an infinite range of opinion. But all this does not create the connection from which we can become grounded.[7]

In a world enhanced by the Internet, human touch seems less necessary. One Microsoft Windows Phone commercial depicts

---

7. Peter Block, *Community: The Structure of Belonging* (San Francisco: Berrett-Koehler Publishers, 2008), 1–2.

men and women in various situations with their faces buried in their handheld devices. Meanwhile, the people around them get disgusted and shout, "Really!" Connecting via digital social media is great, but our bodies still matter. Genuine eye contact can never be replaced by a click or a touch on our electronic devices. An actual smile warms the heart more than a slew of emoticons.

Road Rule 4 Beware of being overly critical of new media, and don't assume it cannot contribute to healthy relationships and communities. Explore and understand how these media connect people and build community, even as you become aware of their limits.

Jesus as the Ultimate Medium

Christians actually have a special handle on media and technology, especially as tools for connecting people in an increasingly fragmented world. It all comes down to the Incarnation. Here is how we see it:

In communication, media (singular: medium) are the tools to store and deliver information or data. In Christianity, we understand Jesus to be the chief medium for God. As the Gospel of John says:

> [T]he Word became flesh and lived among us, and we have seen his glory, the glory as of a father's only son, full of grace and truth. (John 1:14)

Anyone who wants to be intimate and connected with the almighty God who created the universe, can now turn to this medium, Jesus, and discover the glory and truth of God.

This brings us to the concept of incarnation: God is now accessible and present, literally in-carnate (in the flesh) through Jesus Christ. The Episcopal Way for many begins with the moment of incarnation, when the Holy Spirit dwelt in Mary and she gave birth to Jesus, also called Immanuel, or God with us, and the course of human existence changed forever. People needed a medium, some way of capturing the divine essence of

incarnation: God dwelling among us, in the flesh, through Jesus Christ

God and connecting us to God. We received it in Jesus.

That explains why sacraments are so important for Episcopalians. A sacrament is a visible, physical sign of the still-lively presence of Jesus, usually housed in a ritual like baptism or communion, both moments when we believe Jesus shows up to meet his followers. In other words, a sacrament is also a medium, delivering the presence of Jesus to us. To be a sacramental Christian is to assume Jesus shows up in a variety of rituals, modes, and people. He did not shun flesh and blood when he became human, and he is still willing to come among us in order to show the way to God's own heart.

Thomas Cranmer, the author of the English language Prayer Book and father of Anglicanism, painted this word-picture to explain the power of incarnation and sacraments:

> Our Savior Christ hath not only set forth these things most plainly in his holy word, that we may hear them with our ears, but he has also ordained one visible sacrament of spiritual regeneration in water [*baptism*], and another visible sacrament of spiritual nourishment in bread and wine [*communion*], to the intent that, as much as is possible for man, we may see Christ with our eyes, smell him at our nose, taste him with our mouths, grope him with our hands, and perceive him with all our senses.[8]

Cranmer lovingly describes how we touch, taste, and smell Jesus Christ, and via Jesus, touch, taste, and smell God. Few sacraments communicate that intimacy more powerfully or regular-

---

8. Thomas Cranmer, "Answer to the Book of M. Stephen Gardiner, Late Bishop of Winchester," as reprinted in Richard Schmidt, *Glorious Companions* (Grand Rapids, MI: Eerdmans Publishing, 2002), 10.

sacrament: a visible, physical sign of the presence and power of Jesus, usually accessed via a ritual like baptism or communion

ly than the Eucharist. Literally the "Great Thanksgiving," Eucharist is the table fellowship, the Holy Communion, where we share bread and wine that have been blessed, and give thanks for the mysterious way that Jesus meets us in these gifts.

The first letter to the Christian community in Corinth records the words and the promise we still recall whenever we gather at table for Communion:

> The Lord Jesus on the night when he was betrayed took a loaf of bread, and when he had given thanks, he broke it and said, "This is my body that is for you. Do this in remembrance of me." In the same way he took the cup also, after supper, saying, "This cup is the new covenant in my blood. Do this, as often as you drink it, in remembrance of me." For as often as you eat this bread and drink the cup, you proclaim the Lord's death until he comes. (1 Corinthians 11:23–26)

Eucharist may be one of the most peculiar things Christians do, compared to other faith traditions—does anyone else dare to consume the flesh and blood of their God? And yet this is the main worship service for Episcopalians. If you ask why we are so deeply invested in this ritual, it comes back to the conviction that, in this moment, we are truly receiving Jesus' body and being knit together as a body. Then we are sent into the world, full of grace and truth, not just to talk about Jesus and his good news, but to *be* the body of Jesus, bringing the peace, good news, and healing he promised. It comes back to the incarnation—our flesh has become his (and his ours), and our lives belong to him.

Another way to understand this is that we become media for God. If Jesus was the principal medium, by partaking in sacraments like Baptism and Eucharist, we become part of the body of Christ, and thus become media for the incarnate Christ. Could it be that we are the original social media?

Hardwired for Connection

Episcopalians are hardwired to appreciate the role of media in growing authentic connections. We believe God wants to be with us, and that God initiates this relationship via Jesus, the Word of God made flesh. We also trust that God is speaking and growing relationship with us via the other Word of God: the Bible.

Some five hundred years ago, King Henry VIII embraced the radical technology known as the printing press and used it to print the Great Bible in English. It is almost impossible for anyone alive today to grasp what a revolution this was. Before John Wycliffe translated the Bible in 1382, the scriptures were only available in Latin or ancient languages (those who attempted to translate it into common languages were routinely excommunicated or killed). Before William Tyndale's version was published and printed in 1526, the Word of God was only held by a few specially trained professionals or underground faithful.

Henry intended the publication of the Bible to fracture support for the Roman Catholic Church and shore up his church in England; it also fanned the flames of Protestant Reformation in the kingdom. The first Book of Common Prayer in 1549 propelled that revolution another giant step forward. Through the medium of the printed book, laypeople gained unprecedented access to all the worship services (liturgies) of the church, the Psalms, and prayers for private use and public gatherings. At the time of that printing, most people could not read, but those who could were able to take up the stories and prayers and feel close to God in a way they never had before.

There is a reason why Episcopalians are known as "People of the Book." To this day, the Book of Common Prayer empowers communities to worship and connect to each other, to the church past and present, and most importantly to God. It places the

Book of Common Prayer: the book of the church's worship services, plus the Psalms, prayers, and (later) the church's historical documents and teachings

words of faith in the people's hands, so that each of us can share faith and hope wherever we go.

These media—Bible and Prayer Book—communicate the life and truth of God, draw people together, and form us into mediums of the holy. But maybe, if we are to assist our digitized world in finding the blessings of digital life, we should expand the scope and call ourselves "People of the Media." We could explore the way new media can knit together authentic, flesh-and-blood communities in the present and future. We could partner with digital natives to honor their knowledge and experience, while challenging them (and ourselves) to maximize the use of the digital media to foster faithful communities that can see, hear, taste, and touch Christ.

Is this good news to a world where digital media increasingly facilitate human interaction? We think it is. Following the Episcopal Way, we trust that books, iPhones, tablets, Twitter, Instagram, and a host of formats and devices we cannot today imagine could be essential tools for growing Christian community and union with God. We also know the power of face-to-face contact, and that nothing is more sacramental and grace filled than flesh and blood, water, and bread and wine. And when we lose touch with that truth, the Episcopal Way sends us out to be the media through whom God speaks and heals and invites people close to God once again.

TRY THIS   Talk to a "digital native" and ask how they experience community through social media. If you are a digital native, ask the same question of a friend who is not part of a church. And if you are not part of a faith community already, then consider how social media and the Internet both facilitate and detract from community for you.

Chapter 4

A Multi-Tasking World and a Liturgical Church

Eric once showed his two-year-old grandniece a cool app on his iPad that he thought (hoped) would occupy her attention for a while. Within one minute, she knew exactly which button to push to get out of the app. With another stroke and a touch, she opened the app she really wanted to play with . . . not that it kept her occupied much longer.

Multi-tasking, short attention span, impatience, and constant interruptions are part of the new world reality, and not just for youth. As Eric and Stephanie collaborated on this book, both of us jumped from one chapter to another. During long Skype conversations, writing into the same document simultaneously on Google Drive, we both periodically checked email and texted (Eric managed to check Facebook, too). We made suggestions for important material to include in the previous or a later chapter, and cut and pasted material from the web or other sources directly into documents for the other to consider.

The tech-savvy, media-driven contexts we both move in affirm this non-linear, multi-track way of thinking. But it makes you wonder: What are all these inputs and shifts doing to the twenty-first-century brain?

Nicholas Carr poses the same question in *The Shallows: What the Internet Is Doing to Our Brains*. His observation: "As our window onto the world, and onto ourselves, a popular medium molds what we see and how we see it—and eventually, if we use it enough, it changes who we are, as individuals and as a society."[9]

Gaining or Losing Our Minds?

In one of his seemingly random web hunts, Eric happened upon an infographic[10] called "How Social Media Is Ruining Our Minds." It opens like this:

Are you accustomed to receiving your news in 140 characters? Watching videos in under 10 minutes? If so, you may be changing *the way your brain works.* Studies show that *social media has a profound effect on the human mind,* something we should all be aware of.

© Assisted Living Today: assistedlivingtoday.com/p/
resources/social-media-is-ruining-our-minds-infographic

---

9. Nicholas Carr, *The Shallows: What the Internet Is Doing to Our Brains* (New York: W.W. Norton, 2010), 3.

10. An infographic pairs various images (graphics) with slices of related information (info). This one was created by Assisted Living Today. See it here: assistedlivingtoday.com/p/resources/social-media-is-ruining-our-minds-infographic

The infographic then passes along some powerful and surprising facts about how technology may be changing our brains. Here are just a few:

Speeding Life Up: Much has been said about our increasing impatience, and much of it is attributed to the fact that everything is instantly available to us these days.

Attention Span: The average attention span at present is just 5 minutes long. Ten years ago, it was 12 minutes. That's a pretty drastic change.

Effects of a Shortened Attention Span: 25% forget the names or details of close friends and even relatives. 7% of people forget their own birthdays from time to time. In the UK last year £1.6 billion of damage was caused by lack of concentration.

Interruptions: Every time we start a new task, the brain has to reorient itself. [Yet] the average office worker checks his email inbox 30–40 times an hour. Nearly once every 1.5 minutes!

Rewiring Our Brains: Brains are constantly changing and adapting, according to our experiences. They don't just sit there in our heads, but grow and adjust. A UCLA study showed that just 5 hours of Internet surfing can change the way your brain works.

Social Media/Internet Addiction Is Real: Students asked to give up media for 24 hours had the following symptoms: phantom phone vibrations (reaching for a phone that wasn't there) and fidgeting and restlessness.

This is the way of the world, especially for people who have grown up with television, video games, laptops, and smart phones. It has its blessings . . . and its shadow side. For instance, we have instant access to information from an endless variety of sources. But who can slow down enough to ask critical questions or dig into sources that don't affirm our original opinions?

Likewise, the ability to multi-task, draw outside the lines, and think in both image and word is an asset for problem solving and decision making. It also detracts from our ability to concentrate and delve deeply into any single topic or moment. And have we mentioned that it's simply exhausting to have everything shifting, everyone speaking, everything visible? When does it stop?

Road Rule 5 The next time the phone rings or you get a text while you're busy with another task, pause. Can it wait? Chances are, the answer is yes.

The Stillpoint

Ask an Episcopalian what's the most important part of being in this church, and chances are very good that you will hear one word: liturgy. Meanwhile, in evangelical Protestant circles, leaders are publishing books and writing articles about this foreign phenomenon called "the liturgy" and how to weave it into their more verbal and linear worship forms. They're also showing up at the doorsteps of liturgical churches to pray and learn by our side.

What is it that people across the spectrum are finding? We believe it has everything to do with the way the liturgy speaks into—and helps to balance—our multi-tasking, image-soaked, non-stop nation.

First, a clarifying word on "the liturgy," a loaded phrase that means different things all at once. The word *leitourgia* is Greek for any private offering or work intended for use by the public. Wealthy ancient Greeks built bridges and roads and hosted rituals knowing they would not be the only ones to benefit—it was their work (often at great cost) on behalf of the people. That's why you will often hear Episcopalians say liturgy is "the work of the people"). Technically, all public worship is liturgy: a public offering or work done by a subset for the sake of the many.

And yet, certain churches are known as "liturgical": the Orthodox, Roman Catholic, Anglican, Lutheran, among others. What unites us is the way our worship falls within a fairly common frame, developed by the fourth century:

liturgy: any worship service, usually built on a historic pattern of worship

- Gathering (music, prayer)
- Proclamation (scriptures and sermon)
- Prayers of the People
- Peace
- Offering
- Communion (or Liturgy of the Table)
- Final Prayer and Dismissal

Even within that frame, you will hear echoes in most liturgical church services, especially when they come to the table for Communion. For instance, we generally begin Eucharist with this greeting, which traces to the first worship book, the Apostolic Tradition of Hippolytus:

Presider	The Lord be with you.
People	And also with you. (or "And with your spirit.")
Presider	Lift up your hearts.
People	We lift them up to the Lord.
Presider	Let us give thanks to the Lord our God.
People	It is right to give God thanks and praise.
	(or "It is meet and right.")

For Episcopalians and our brother and sister Anglicans around the world, the links are even closer. We all derive our liturgy from the first Book of Common Prayer penned in 1549 (which itself drew on many common Catholic and Orthodox sources). The prayers and intentions of Thomas Cranmer and early Anglicans continue to guide and inspire our worship globally.

Of course, you won't find Anglicans in Nigeria and Birmingham using exactly the same words as counterparts in New York or

Ireland. The Prayer Book accommodates a degree of local adaptation so that the Word of God rings true and clear in the actual communities where we worship, live, and serve. But we're all tracing to common roots in the Book of Common Prayer, all beholden to a common, stable form.

In Episcopal liturgy, as we see in the outline above, there is generally a time for listening and responding to scripture; a time to pray for the world, the church, the community, and individuals' needs, and to give thanks and confess our sins; a time for offering the peace of Christ to each other; a time to offer ourselves and our resources for ministry; a time for blessing the bread and wine and re-presenting the body and blood of Christ; and a time to be sent into the world to serve one another and God. Many of these elements are adaptable, which guarantees that the local expressions can vary from one Episcopal church to another. But the common form—plus rubrics or rules for worship that are unique to the Episcopal Church—mean you can recognize the shared Episcopal Way wherever you roam.

The liturgy provides followers of the Episcopal Way with a stillpoint in a world that is sorely lacking in consistency and touchstones. Our families and friends are scattered, our job security has vanished, and even the products we depend on disappear overnight because now there's a "new-and-improved formula!!" With nonstop innovation and interruption, multiple inputs, and information overload so extreme they are changing our brains—we could all use something that is deeply rooted, something that was not created last year (or even in the last century) and will likely still be around long after we're gone.

Multi-Sensory Church for a Multi-Tasking Culture

But a consistent liturgy isn't worth much if it does not speak to the rest of our lives. Episcopal liturgy is multi-sensory and multi-focused—it can engage our multi-tasking, short-attention-spanned brains and bring us closer to God.

That may explain why people born in the 1980s and 1990s (known as Millennials) have begun to quietly turn toward liturgical traditions in surprising numbers. Gracy Olmstead wrote about the trend in *American Conservative* magazine and sparked a flurry of articles and blog posts. She noticed that, "Rather than abandoning Christianity, some young people are joining more traditional, liturgical denominations—notably the Roman Catholic, Anglican, and Orthodox branches of the faith. This trend is deeper than denominational waffling: it's a search for meaning that goes to the heart of our postmodern age."[11]

Stephanie founded and led an alternative worship community called The Crossing, where young leaders worked together to translate Episcopal liturgy for their vibrant downtown Boston neighborhood. She saw hundreds of people like the ones Olmstead studied, all of them discovering a multi-sensory, engaging liturgy that connected them to God in new ways. One young woman, Kirsten, shared her story for the book *Ancient Faith, Future Mission*:

> For most of my life, church has been a place where people multitasked. At my grandparents' church in Ohio, I could look down the pew and see my great-uncle balancing his checkbook, my mother filling in the picture on the front of the bulletin, maybe even someone nodding off in the corner. . . .
>
> It took me more than a year of being a member of The Crossing community to realize that it had never once occurred to me to pull out a pen and draw flowers in the margins of my worship sheet. Because my whole self was being wholly engaged in worship and community, I did not have the time or the brain space or the distracted urge to multi-task. For me this was the freshest kind of church experience—a kind of worship where I was being asked

---

11. Gracy Olmstead, "Why Millennials Long for Liturgy: Is the High Church the Christianity of the Future?" *American Conservative,* January 14, 2014.

to respond and participate and bring my whole self to be, in that moment and that place, in relationship with God and fellow followers of Christ.[12]

Kirsten discovered what liturgical churches have held out for more than a thousand years, and it captured her roaming attention as nothing else could. Along the Episcopal Way, she experienced the incarnation in action. Smell the incense and flowers. Walk toward the altar. Gaze up into the vaulted cathedral ceiling. Shake hands at the Passing of the Peace. Feel the low rumble of the organ. Move to the beat of the drum. Taste the bread on your tongue. Feel the wine flow down your throat. Listen to the voices lifted in praise. Join the body of Christ in motion and in stillness.

The world around us is not likely to slow or simplify anytime soon. If we want to operate differently, to be fully present and loving and not as frazzled and fragmented as the dominant culture seems to demand, we will need some help. The Episcopal Way could be the answer to a prayer: embracing the energy and intensity of multi-taskers, and channeling it into the consistent, beautiful, and grounded form known as the liturgy.

TRY THIS   Open the Book of Common Prayer. (Don't have one? Go to www.bcponline.org.) Turn to the section of prayers called "Collects." Find one that speaks to your life or sounds like the conversation you want to have with God right now, and pray it whenever you think of it: for the day, or a week. Imagine others are praying with you—they are.

---

12. Graham Cray, Ian Mobsby, and Stephanie Spellers, eds., *Ancient Faith, Future Mission: Fresh Expressions in the Sacramental Tradition* (New York: Church Publishing, 2010), 144–45.

Chapter 5

Network Theory and a Networked Church

Nature has known it all along: relationship determines everything. An idea or a system does not simply exist; it emerges from a context, from its relationship to the life around it. When it dies, it does not disappear; rather, it becomes the source of new life. Why? Because everything is connected.

When new structures or ideas occur, they do not rise from nothingness or a single individual's brainstorm. The various elements work together, influence each other up close and from a distance, until the whole system makes a leap. Why? Because everything is connected.

Scientists had been making observations like this for generations, but Fritjof Capra upped the ante in 1975 with *The Tao of Physics,* an underground classic about quantum physics and life systems. For the next few decades, thinkers in the natural sciences, social sciences, philosophy, and religion made their own quantum leaps. Together, they facilitated a shift from seeing the universe as a machine or closed system with rules, regulations, and externally controlled parts toward a view that is more dynamic, interconnected, and participatory.

Living in a Networked World

That wisdom might have been somewhat controversial in the 1970s or even the 1990s. Today, the presence and power of networks is a given. Nicholas Christakis and James Fowler, in their book, *Connected,* take a closer look at just why all those networks make such a difference:

> Social networks have value precisely because they help us to achieve what we could not achieve on our own. . . . [N]etworks influence the spread of joy, the search for sexual partners, the maintenance of health, the functioning of markets, and the struggle for democracy. Yet, social-network effects are not always positive. Depression, obesity, sexually transmitted diseases, financial panic, violence, and even suicide also spread. Social networks, it turns out, tend to magnify whatever they are seeded with.[13]

Through their research on social networks, Christakis and Fowler describe the "Rules of Life in the Network" as follows:

- We shape our network.
- Our network shapes us.
- Our friends affect us.
- Our friends' friends' friends affect us.
- The network has a life of its own.[14]

Christakis and Fowler advance the theory of "three degrees of influence"—in short, what we do or say can impact our friends (first degree), our friends' friends (second degree), and our friends'

---

13. Nicholas Christakis and James Fowler, *Connected: The Surprising Power of Our Social Networks and How They Shape Our Lives* (New York: Hachette Book Group, 2009), 30–31.

14. Ibid., 16–36.

friends' friends (third degree). Used strategically and effectively, the network has tremendous power. [15]

Take the example of Wikipedia, one of the best cases of leveraging relationships for a common good. In that complex, orderly, yet self-organizing system, a whole network of people gathers to share resources and accomplish a shared passion and vision. Thanks to the flexibility and wisdom of the network, the structure can shift as the needs and conditions shift. The various roles in the system can shift as the structure shifts. Leadership can be identified and appointed as it becomes necessary. The result is an encyclopedia more comprehensive and arguably more accurate than the centralized, non-networked Britannica model.

The Light and Shadow of Emergence

In the last 20 years, that wisdom has begun to shape a new breed of church. Alternately called emergent, missional, fresh expressions, or mission-shaped, these ministries are linked by their commitment to listen deeply to a context and then grow relationships between ever-widening circles of people who share a passion. The network model in these churches influences everything; the structure and roles and worship forms are determined by the community and its network as they listen for God's Spirit. It's a much more fluid and nimble form than the one you'll find in conventional churches, and it may be truer to the emergent spirit swirling in the world around us.

Could there be a shadow side to something so intuitive and effective? Indeed, there is. Stephanie has worked for years with congregations in the emergent movement, some of which describe themselves as "network or affinity-based" communities. They may or may not share a location, but what counts is that they

---

15. Ibid., 26–30.

share an affinity. You can imagine how quickly such ministries become segregated. Even when more people are showing up, it may simply be more like-minded people. The drive to connect and collaborate based chiefly on passions and shared interests, without actively shaping or correcting self-segregating habits, can create self-affirming, limited-set circles.

Road Rule 6 Pay as much attention to wisdom and perspectives beyond your group as you do to those within it. Keep your circle and your ears open.

The other shadow is a tendency to privilege the now, to see the contemporary context as the only one that matters. If a piece of wisdom is not already present in your affinity group, if it is not within those crucial three degrees of separation, how will you find it? The group needs to reach ahead into the future and around to contemporaries, but also backward, mining for some wisdom it did not generate for itself.

There is at least one more shadow: The network can be used consciously and unconsciously to spread fear, propagate hate, isolate and control others, and break down communities. For example, we have witnessed political parties of every stripe spreading misinformation through official and underground networks. Not every network is mobilized for the greater good.

A Radically Connected Church

Two thousand years ago, Jesus initiated an extraordinary network with these words: "You will receive power when the Holy Spirit has come upon you; and you will be my witnesses in Jerusalem, in all Judea and Samaria, and to the ends of the earth" (Acts 1:8).

He sent apostles out as his representatives, first locally (to Jerusalem) and then to nearby towns and communities (Samaria), and ultimately to the ends of the earth. His movement spread without the help of the Internet, and was eventually embraced by the weak and powerful, young and old, men and women, making Christianity the most popular religion in Europe for more than a millennium.

> **Nicene Creed:** a statement of faith in God as Father, Son, and Holy Spirit, affirmed by the Council of Constantinople in 381 and recited in most Episcopal churches on Sundays

Jesus understood the power of networks, and the Episcopal Way affirms it. At the widest level, we speak of the relationship with the body of Christ or the communion of saints. This is the community of every Christian—past, present, and future.

Episcopalians are also part of the body of Christians throughout the ages who share a common catholic heritage. Remember: when we say we are "catholic with a small c," it is not just a statement regarding brothers and sisters in the Roman Catholic Church. Being a catholic Christian means you are part of a universal church, one that embraces a variety of cultures, regions, and perspectives.

Churches that share this heritage turn to the Nicene Creed, a statement of faith affirmed by the first Council of Constantinople in 381 and recited in most Episcopal churches on Sundays. Toward the close of the Creed, members declare: "We believe in *one, holy, catholic,* and *apostolic* church."

- *One* describes the unity of the church under Christ.

- *Holy* means being set apart for God's purpose.

- *Catholic* means universal.

- *Apostolic* refers to the continuous line from the earliest Christian leaders, Jesus' apostles, to leaders in this day and age.

This shared statement of faith links us to a network larger than Episcopal or Anglican churches. When we speak it, our voices join with billions of Christians over the ages.

Telescope a bit closer and you see the network of Christians known as the Anglican Communion. This is the 77 million people around the world who share roots in the Church of England and together create indigenous (or local) expressions of the Anglican Way. The Episcopal Church is one of several provinces, or more or less national churches, within the Anglican Communion.

Then there is the network of the Episcopal Church, which actually embraces churches in the United States and thirteen other countries where we founded Anglican communities with the particular flavor and structure of the Episcopal Church.

Ultimately, we come to the network that is the congregation. You cannot be a Christian without gathering, living, serving, praying, and breaking bread with a group of fellow travelers. Christian life depends on the network.

Consider this: Many other Protestant Christians would say the basic unit of Christian community is the congregation, the one they attend on a Sunday morning, the one that baptized their children, buried their parents. Those congregations may have connections to other churches—in a conference, in an assembly—but the relationship that matters most to their members is the one with their local circle.

For Episcopalians—at least according to our Constitution and Canons—the basic unit of Christian community is a diocese. That is the organized body of churches in an area, sometimes a state (like the Diocese of Nevada), sometimes related areas in a state (like the Diocese of Northern California, one of six dioceses within that state), in special situations a whole country (like the Diocese of Haiti or the Dominican Republic), or even a geographic region (like the Episcopal churches in Europe). They share a bishop, who is elected by the people to serve as a pastor, teacher, leader in mission, and—you guessed it—the main representative for the diocese as it relates to other dioceses.

If I am Episcopalian, I do not just belong to St. Paul's by the Sea, the one with the red door and the 150-year-old organ and the bell choir. I belong to a diocese, which means I am guaranteed to be connected to a network of people,

diocese: the organized body of Episcopal churches in an area, led by a bishop

some of whom I would almost surely not choose. Eric is in the Diocese of Los Angeles, which ties together All Saints Church in Beverly Hills, a wealthy and vibrant church with Hollywood movers and shakers; Holy Spirit in Silver Lake, an emergent church in a café; and St. James in the City, whose Korean drummers shake the church's foundations. Stephanie serves in the Diocese of Long Island, which stretches from the mixture of humanity who live near the Brooklyn Bridge, through the United Nations-like community that is Queens, into suburban Nassau County, and out to the seclusion and privilege of the Hamptons. What reality can hold all these worlds together? Only a diocese.

bishop: the elected clergy person with oversight (Latin: *episcope*) of a diocese, who serves as pastor, teacher, leader in mission, and connector to the wider church

TRY THIS Visit four Episcopal churches near you on several Sundays. Look closely at the worship, architecture, and community life and then take notes:

- What similarities link these churches?
- What differences separate them?
- How do they seem to understand being Episcopal? (It's good to ask!)

Why would we choose to live networked like this? It's all about the power of relationships. Together, we can share resources so everyone can live out God's mission: resources like money, people, knowledge, skills, and buildings. If I have a bright idea and we are in relationship, my dream may connect with your great need and still another person's gifts, and a whole new ministry is possible.

While we live in specific, local contexts where we share love, healing, and ministry, these broader networks can provide resources and support for local expressions. For example, the Episcopal Church Women, one of the oldest and strongest networks in the Episcopal Church, collects donations from almost every Episcopal Church, via the United Thank Offering (you can find their little blue paper boxes at the entrance to lots of churches).

In 2013, the United Thank Offering distributed more than $1.5 million through forty-eight grants, to support projects like building a community hall in Burundi, creating gardens in Arkansas, making a film about bullying, and improving the health of mothers and children in Haiti. This cross-church, voluntary network teaches us the extraordinary power of connection. We can choose to use our relationships to share helpful information, speak truth, build trust, and develop communities that act for love and justice.

It's the Network

As so often comes with power, when Christianity became the dominant religion in the fourth century, we too often used our networks to enforce rules, control communities, and consolidate power into a few hands. That dominant network has begun to crumble, especially in its old strongholds in Europe and North America. In our changing world, where networked living is a given, the Episcopal Way has a chance to reinitiate Jesus' charge to be his witnesses through our networks, locally and globally.

I am an Episcopalian because I connect with a local and global network of people who follow Christ, emphasize mutual respect among people, share the Word and sacraments, and share resources to create communities of transformative love and hope everywhere. As a Christian, I accept the responsibility of being only one degree of separation from God through Jesus Christ. Spiritually, I am part of a network of holy women and men who stretch back two thousand years or longer.

When we are networked like this, and we share faith in this big and diverse circle, the life and holy love that emerge are so much fuller and truer than anything we could have created alone or even in a local congregation. Mother Nature had it right: life is better within the network.

TRY THIS List five people who you consider friends with whom you have regular interactions. Who is in your network? How did you meet? What do you have in common, and how are they different from you?

Now consider how each of these friends has influenced you and how you have influenced them in the last year. What gifts have you received from your friends' networks and what gifts from your own networks can you offer your friends?

Do the same exercise looking around your church, if you are a member of one:

- Who is in your church?
- How did you all get there?
- What do you have in common, and what is different?
- What have you received from this congregation?
- What could you share with this church that would make new or existing ministries flourish?

Chapter 6

Flattened Authority and a Democratic Church

Once upon a time, leadership equaled the exercise of power, usually from the top down. The leader cast a vision and issued orders; the people further down the chain implemented orders. Sometimes those mid-level managers made decisions appropriate to their level and passed them to the people below them. Overall, the goal was to follow what came from on high and not screw up.

You will see a very different system at work in companies like Google and Toyota. These organizations are not rife with anarchy; there is too much money and too much responsibility at stake for that. But the structures and order tend to be more fluid (see the previous chapter on networks); they have built in a host of mechanisms to facilitate participation, collaboration, on-site decision making, idea generation, and feedback at every level.

If you think that is only happening in hip companies and political campaigns, think again. It is even changing the most regimented structure imaginable: the military. Stephanie was sitting at a table full of innovative leaders, discussing hopes for new structures and ways to exercise authority, when a colleague mentioned *It's Your Ship: Management Techniques from the Best Damn Ship in the Navy*, by Captain D. Michael Abrashoff. She immediately wondered: Why do I want tips from some military guy? Perhaps because he was right.

When Abrashoff took control of the U.S.S. Benfold in 1997, he drew the logical conclusion that there was no way he could make every decision. He wasn't trying to be a revolutionary, simply a realist. He trained people to think and make judgments on their own. Of course, the officers around him balked, because they had only been taught to follow orders. No one knew how to take the lead alongside other leaders. Here is what he told them:

> I chose my line in the sand. Whenever the consequences of a decision had the potential to kill or injure someone, waste taxpayers' money, or damage the ship, I had to be consulted. Short of those contingencies, the crew was authorized to make their own decisions. Even if the decisions were wrong, I would stand by them.[16]

As a result of this change, his crew went from being the worst in the Pacific Fleet to the best in the Navy. People knew they were trusted, knew they had a voice, and that knowledge made them more connected, more invested, more loyal, and just plain better at everything they did. Captain Abrashoff still had a job and clearly held plenty of power, but the structure was far less centralized. Instead, he came to see, "My job was to create the climate that enabled people to unleash their potential. Given the right environment, there are few limits to what people can achieve."[17] He had power, and he knew what to do with it: share it, so that people could discover their own power and then work together toward the common goal.

It is not so different from the inner workings of an ant colony: the queen does not give orders to the ants. Each one senses what's happening in its environment, acts accordingly, and leaves a chemi-

---

16. D. Michael Abrashoff, *It's Your Ship: Management Techniques from the Best Damn Ship in the Navy* (New York: Hachette Book Group, 2002), 27.

17. Ibid., 29.

cal trail that acts as a stimulus to other ants. An extraordinarily complex system solves all manner of problems—where to bury a dead ant, how to build the hill, how to transport food where it's needed most—all without a command-and-control official at the top.

The New Normal

Flattened authority is practically a given among people born after 1965. They expect to share authority, to participate, and to have their voices heard. When they engage conventional systems framed by a more hierarchical paradigm, they are often deeply frustrated by the promise of conversation and collaboration and the reality of command-and-control systems.

What happens when these alternative leadership structures have the chance to work in the real world? We have already mentioned the example of Wikipedia, the crowd-sourced encyclopedia that is now a first stop for learning about almost any topic. You could also turn to the example of Occupy, the worldwide movement born when thousands of people, most under the age of 40, occupied sections of Wall Street back in 2011 to protest systems that keep most of the wealth and power in the hands of the "One Percent."

Occupy camps across the country and around the world became communities living out a social experiment: food and resources were shared within the group, there were rarely designated leaders for outside groups to focus on, decisions were made via consensus, and everyone's voice had an opportunity to be heard.

Occupy looked like a mess from the outside and, on the inside, where Stephanie served as a chaplain to protesters in Boston, it often was. But it was also one of the most empowering and authentic communities many participants had known. When Superstorm Sandy hit the greater New York area, Occupy Wall Street morphed into Occupy Sandy and deployed a nimble, responsive, self-regenerating relief and recovery effort. They were so successful even the Federal Emergency Management Agency (FEMA) sent officials to Occupy meetings, to learn, to borrow their superior training, and to consult Occupy for ground updates.[18] Flattened authority was, for the moment, vindicated.

Road Rule 7 The next time you are in a room full of people at different levels of power, try listening to and honoring the people with less power. Assume every person is a child of God and has within them the spirit and wisdom of Christ.

The blessings of flattened authority are many. So are the shadows. For instance, Occupy's greatest strength—maximum democratic participation—also proved to be one of its greatest weaknesses. With so many voices carrying equal weight, Occupiers often found they were churning and churning but going nowhere. The hyper-democratic model failed to recognize that some individuals brought specific expertise that needed to be trusted and even privileged. Especially in the face-off with financial powers, Occupy could send out statements, rallies filled the streets, but it was incredibly difficult for the group to make the kinds of changes participants clearly longed for. Everyone had power to go their individual way, which meant the group itself lacked the power to move as a cohesive unit and make lasting change.

A Democratic Church

When the Church of England was transplanted to American shores, it brought a command-and-control, royal system to the Colonies. Luckily, some of the same people who gave concrete form to the new American republic also put their heads together

---

18. "Where FEMA Fell Short, Occupy Was There," *New York Times* (November 9, 2012) and "Occupy Sandy Emerges as Relief Organization for 21st Century, Mastering Social Networks," *Huffington Post* (November 5, 2012).

General Convention: the every-three-years gathering of Episcopal leaders (bishops, clergy, laity) who craft major policy and set direction for the whole church

to form a new Anglican expression in the United States: the Episcopal Church.

America was a democratic nation. So the Episcopal Church would be a democratic church. Americans certainly would not pledge allegiance to the English crown. The first American Prayer Book removed that vow from the priestly ordination service. American lawmakers met in two houses: a House of Representatives (the larger and wider body) and a Senate House (a smaller body with more senior members). Eventually the Episcopal Church's leaders began to gather and make decisions at a national General Convention in two chambers, as well: a House of Deputies (made up of priests, deacons, and non-ordained people [the laity] elected by each diocese) and a House of Bishops (all bishops currently serving, plus retired bishops who generally speak but do not vote).

To this day, the Episcopal system of electing our own bishops baffles the rest of the Anglican Communion. In 2003, the people of the Diocese of New Hampshire gathered for a Convention to elect a bishop. Having already spent months in discernment and preparation, they chose Gene Robinson, an out gay man in a partnered relationship. Our church's counterparts around the world cried foul, because in their systems a bishop would be selected by senior authorities and then placed in a diocese. How could the American church leaders force a gay bishop on the people of New Hampshire? How could the bishops, who are keenly aware of their relationship to the worldwide church, make a move guaranteed to anger Anglicans elsewhere?

The only answer we could offer was to explain our system of voting: the people elected Robinson to serve as their chief pastor, teacher, and leader in mission. After that, the rest of the Episcopal Church could offer consent or reject him, but the default was to honor the decision by the people on the ground. That is what it means to be a democratic church.

Common Prayer for Common People

To be sure, democracy is also in our DNA as Anglicans. As we have already discussed, Thomas Cranmer filled the first Prayer Book with scriptures and printed the texts of all the services of the church. He literally created a prayer book for common people, in the common language, so that all people could pray in common. Maybe that is why so many Episcopalians point with reverence to the Book of Common Prayer.

We pray in common; we also listen for and trust the voices of the common people. In the Outline of the Faith in the Book of Common Prayer (it is also called the Catechism, though it is in no way as authoritative as the teachings or confessions you would find in churches like the Roman Catholic, Lutheran, or Presbyterian), we pose the question: *Who are the ministers of the church?* Answer: *The ministers of the church are laypersons, bishops, priests, and deacons.*[19] True, we have professional, ordained ministers. But the primary group of ministers is the one listed first: laypersons.

Few contemporary leaders understood this better than Verna Dozier. A laywoman and school teacher turned theologian, she kept the Episcopal Church true to its democratic call. She once wrote: "There are no second-class citizens in the household of God. Religious authority comes with baptism, and it is nurtured by prayer, worship, bible study, life together."[20] She knew that every baptized person in the Episcopal Church is called to be a minister.

The Baptismal Covenant spells out the calling of the baptized with specificity and power. A unique Episcopal contribution to the Anglican tradition, the covenant is found on pages 304–305 of the Book of Common Prayer. It climaxes with

Baptismal Covenant: the set of promises made by all baptized Episcopalians, which we keep with God's help

---

19. "An Outline of the Faith," Book of Common Prayer, 855.

20. Verna Dozier, *The Calling of the Laity* (Washington, DC: Alban Institute, 1988), 115.

the five queries to those being baptized (or to the people making promises on their behalf, if the baptized are children):

Celebrant	Will you continue in the apostles' teaching and fellowship, in the breaking of bread, and in the prayers?
People	I will, with God's help.
Celebrant	Will you persevere in resisting evil, and, whenever you fall into sin, repent and return to the Lord?
People	I will, with God's help.
Celebrant	Will you proclaim by word and example the Good News of God in Christ?
People	I will, with God's help.
Celebrant	Will you seek and serve Christ in all persons, loving your neighbor as yourself?
People	I will, with God's help.
Celebrant	Will you strive for justice and peace among all people, and respect the dignity of every human being?
People	I will, with God's help.

In these five promises, Episcopalians commit to follow Jesus in a particular way, to combine their energies in order to join God's mission in the world (again, that mission is to restore all people and all of creation back to our original state of union with God). We would say every Christian—certainly every Episcopalian—is blessed to live that mission every day, everywhere we go. And we travel further in that mission because we go together.

A Not-So Flat Church

All the people are ministers, but the balanced approach of the Episcopal Way creates organizations and structures that help us to move and minister as a body. The ant hill and headless star-fish have a hard time harnessing resources and taking bold steps forward. Our model is closer to the naval ship with a captain like Abrashoff, who uses his authority to inspire, identify, and authorize other leaders.

At their best, our structures provide vision, accountability, and strong communication. A diocese brings bishops, clergy, and lay leaders together, all listening, each offering a different perspective and holding a different power. But ultimately, all that power gets laid at the feet of Jesus, who called together his apostles and told them, "Whoever wants to be first must be last of all and servant of all" (Mark 9:35). The only power that matters is power that serves the people and serves God's mission.

TRY THIS Eric developed a process called Mutual Invitation[21] that ensures everyone in the group will have a voice. Try this process with a group of five to twelve people.

In order to ensure that everyone who wants to share has the opportunity to speak, proceed in the following way:

- The leader or a designated person will share first.
- After that person has spoken, he or she then invites another to share. You need not automatically invite the person next to you.
- After the next person has spoken, that person is given the privilege to invite another to share.
- If you are not ready to share yet, say "I pass for now," and we will invite you to share later on.
- If you don't want to say anything, simply say "pass" and invite another person to share.

Continue in this manner until everyone has been invited.

---

21. See Eric H. F. Law, *The Wolf Shall Dwell with the Lamb* (St. Louis: Chalice Press, 1993), 79–88.

Chapter 7

Globalization and an Indigenous Church

Back in the 1990s, Stephanie was serving as a newspaper reporter in Knoxville, Tennessee. The city had no reason to stand out in the American consciousness: host for the 1982 World's Fair, home of the University of Tennessee Volunteers, minutes away from Oak Ridge National Laboratories. But there is one area where Knoxville shone: at the time, the county had more churches per capita than any in the whole country. It was, statistically speaking, the Buckle of the Bible Belt.

Maybe that is why it became a bona fide news story when a Hindu group purchased an empty Baptist church building and turned it into a temple. The global had become local. The local looked quite global.

The word for this process is globalization: increasing the worldwide exchange of national and cultural resources, which results in greater interdependence between cultures and economies. The International Monetary Fund (itself a child of globalization) names four aspects of globalization: trade of goods and services, investment of capital, migration of people, and dissemination of information (some would also add the environment). Each of these fields affects globalization, and each one is affected by it.

globalization: the increasing, worldwide exchange and morphing of national and cultural resources

Of course, communication, travel, and the global movement of people and ideas are not new. Observe, for instance, the popularity of curry in the West Indies. The English showed up in India, loved curry, and when they traveled to the Caribbean they brought curry (and Indian labor) with them. Now you can't find a Jamaican restaurant without curried chicken, goat and ox.

What is new is the speed of globalization and the degree to which it shapes life in America and around the world. For instance, we have always been a nation of immigrants, with a steady stream of groups from various parts of the globe creating new lives and weaving their story into the larger American one. More recently, the trend has become more complex. Groups are bringing their cultures with the expectation that America will not only absorb them, but that they will change America.

In other words, going back to Knoxville, the Hindus are not just living as quiet, marginalized members of a Christian America. They are building temples next door to the Presbyterians and becoming vocal partners in the American experiment. Civic organizations are calling on the local imam, rabbi, pastor, and priest. White Presbyterian young people are meeting and falling in love with their Hindu schoolmates, and interreligious marriages are nearly the majority, where they once horrified families (before the 1960s, only 20 percent of marriages crossed faith lines).[22]

The breakdown of cultural walls locally only mirrors the shift taking place worldwide. Thanks to air travel and digital communication, ideas bounce from one culture to another so quickly it is hard to trace the origin. In the 1980s, we were surprised at the hunger of Russian teenagers for a pair of $200 Levi's. Now

22. Naomi Schaefer Riley, *'Til Faith Do Us Part: How Interfaith Marriage Is Transforming America* (New York: Oxford University Press, 2013), 6.

dance clubs in Rome thump to the beat of French hip-hop, Iranian revolutionaries rely on phones from Sweden, economic troubles in Japan ripple overnight into Greece, and a company can make all its money and house its employees in America but keep all the proceeds (and the tax address) in Venezuela. Globalization is the name of the game.

Indigenous Culture: The New Endangered Species

As promising as it may be to create global networks that help life to flourish around the globe, the force of globalization is not an unbounded good. It is possible to be so radically open to every cultural influence that a group loses its own unique, indigenous voice. After a while, it may not be animal species that go extinct. It may be local, indigenous cultures incapable of resisting the sheer dominance of global trade, communication, and capital.

When the force of economic and political empire shows up, local cultures hardly stand a chance of maintaining their unique way of life. Indigenous people in the Andes lived for millennia on quinoa, a nearly perfect food offering vitamins, minerals, fiber, and protein. Now people in the region harvest quinoa to ship to gourmet stores throughout the United States, while Andean children growing up today have limited access to the food that sustained their families for millennia.

Alas, some are bound to overreact to that danger, and their leap to block outside influences has created a curse all its own. Think of Chinese officials working to close down or censor citizens' access to Facebook and Google. Think of the "Birthers" who planted myths about President Barack Obama's identity, or the more rabid anti-immigration forces, all of which hope to capitalize on the fear that America is being "taken over" by outside groups. As sands shift and outside cultural influences stir new questions and raise new possibilities, leaders in a particular context may opt for a bunker mentality.

Michiel Schwarz names the great challenge of globalism in his book *Sustainism*: "Finding local identities in a global world beyond the globalization of the local."[23] We could all use some examples of that process lived out fully.

A Catholic Yet Hybrid Church

Few traditions have wrestled to balance these impulses more faithfully or publicly than Anglicanism. To be called Anglican is to love Jesus with others traveling the Anglican Way:

- We shape our prayers after a common form.
- We live in relationship facilitated by our bishops, and connected to the Church of England.
- We return to the Holy Scriptures as the source of our wisdom and life.
- We offer the sacraments of Baptism and Communion.

These four commitments make up the Chicago Quadrilateral, crafted in 1866 to define the connective tissue that links churches across the international Anglican Communion.[24] More important, they map the parameters for what it means to be Anglican. There's no need to become rabid and defensive in the face of cultural change. As long as these marks are present, we know who we are.

And yet, as a global communion, we take flesh or become incarnate in thousands of different cultural contexts, and in most cases that creates a hybrid. Worship in Jamaica and be ready for steel drum bands *and* big organ chorales. Worship in Japan and you will find the stillness of Zen meditation *and* a communion

---

23. Michiel Schwarz and Joost Elffers, *Sustainism* (New York: Distributed Art Publishers, Inc., 2010). From the second to the last chapter titled "Globalization" (*Sustainism* is an art book with no page numbers).

24. "The Chicago-Lambeth Quadrilateral," Book of Common Prayer, 876.

table. Come to New York and find formal, richly textured Anglo-Catholic worship that even the nearby Roman Catholics thought had disappeared—possibly led by a priest from Latin America.

Road Rule 8 When you find you have a passionate preference for one style over another, make an extra effort to explore the story behind your passion. How did you come to this preference? How have others come to theirs? Find ways to affirm and express what you love while respecting different preferences and perspectives.

Nearly every province in the Anglican Communion (most of these networks started as national churches, like the Episcopal Church) has its own prayer book, laws, and practices. In other words, we expect there will be local or indigenous expressions, and that these expressions will shift as the cultures shift. The process grinds along, sometimes painfully, especially when multiple cultures exist in a single locale.

Sometimes we have swung in the direction of locking down our practices and identity markers (more on this in Part III). But at our best, Anglicanism is a hybrid church: Protestant and reformed, yet catholic and ancient; a global church (the Anglican Communion) with local expressions (indigenous).

The Vernacular Principle

Indeed, we have been living this hybrid life all along. Our founders considered it "a thing plainly repugnant to the Word of God, and the custom of the Primitive Church, to have public Prayer in the Church, or to minister the Sacraments in a tongue not understood of the people."[25] How would people speak, much less learn, from

---

25. "Articles of Religion," Book of Common Prayer, 871.

a prayer they could not understand? They needed to celebrate and pray to God using their own indigenous expressions.

We call this truth the Vernacular Principle. It simply states that the language of worship—whether that's a linguistic language, or

Vernacular Principle: the language and expressions of worship should embrace the people's experience and context

a visual or cultural language—should rise from the experience and context in which the people have gathered. The Merriam-Webster Dictionary defines vernacular in this way:

vernacular[26]:
1. using a language or dialect native to a region or country rather than a literary, cultured, or foreign language
2. of, relating to, or being a nonstandard language or dialect of a place, region, or country
3. of, relating to, or being the normal spoken form of a language

The vernacular is roots language, home language, heart language, and it is especially important to groups whose culture has been designated "nonstandard." For instance, Stephanie grew up in the South, where her mother worked as a customer service representative for AT&T. In those days, the telephone giant trained reps to speak standard American English on the telephone. When Stephanie was in her teens, her mother sat her down with some sadness and said, "I'm so sorry." "Why?" Stephanie asked. "I worked so hard making sure you knew the English I speak at work, but I never focused on you learning how black people talk to each other." Her mom was right; Stephanie did not learn the "vernacular"—the nonstandard English dialect of African Americans—until much later.

Vernacular expressions are still entirely related to the "standard," but they reflect the color, flavor, and particularities of a context. Applied to church life, the vernacular is the language—

26. http://www.merriam-webster.com

linguistic, visual, or cultural—that matches the experience and context in which a particular group of people have gathered. Everyone has a vernacular, or "home language"—Texans, Midwesterners, coffee-chugging Seattleites, rural Wyoming farmers, Nuyoricans (the hybrid born at the nexus of New York and Puerto Rico), and Afro-Appalachians. As any of us can tell you, few things are more moving than hearing your church's ancient traditions translated into the language of your home culture(s). Even when your heart sings to the dominant culture, you can be moved at the joy of fellow Episcopalians who long to hear the tradition in the language of their ancestors or neighbors.

Road Rule 9 If the word "evangelism" makes you anxious, think less about convincing someone to believe what you believe and more about growing a relationship. How might this person relate to God? What loves, concerns, and hopes drive their life? How do I talk to God, and what loves, concerns, and hopes drive me? In the process of sharing these stories and growing in understanding, you will already be doing evangelism.

"That Was Loud But Very Anglican"

If we are not adhering to the Vernacular Principle, the church ceases to be faithfully Anglican. To be Anglican is to be in relationship: with our neighborhoods, with the cultures around us. As those conditions on the ground change, we shift with them.

A few years back, Episcopal churches got excited about a liturgy called the U2charist: a service that followed every rule of the Prayer Book but incorporated music from the band U2 and a message geared to raise consciousness about global poverty and health.

About six hundred people attended a U2charist at a General Convention in Anaheim, California, a service both Stephanie and

Eric were happy to attend. As Eric was walking out, he heard an older woman remark, "That was loud . . . but that was very Anglican." The service featured music she had never heard, with dance interludes and screen projections. But she recognized it as an expression rising from the same tradition she claimed. It was a catholic, ancient expression in the vernacular. It was a true Anglican hybrid.

The Episcopal Way has included this kind of adaptation for its entire history. Once upon a time, words like "thee" and "thou" were used on the streets of England but never in church. When the 1979 Book of Common Prayer introduced prayers without these words, and shifted away from the King James translation of the Bible, many people felt we had lost "sacred" or "God" language. In fact, using contemporary American English for our prayers honors the church's deep vernacular tradition.

Everything Is "Glocal"

Globalization causes cultures to rub and bump against each other, and we are bound to find ourselves equally invigorated and agitated. There is always the risk that a dominant culture will wipe out local expressions, and just as much risk that local groups will draw the shutters, hope these emerging cultures will simply disappear, and end up missing a life-giving opportunity.

The vernacular principle introduces a "glocal" path—a combination of the global and the local. We connect globally but express locally. The global Anglican Communion provides essential relationships and resources and the basic contours of faith, but it has rarely sought to control the local or indigenous expressions of the church around the world. Instead, each province is in relationship with its local cultures, helping to give the global Anglican Communion its shape and texture. In the tension and dialogue between the local and the global, the church comes alive in every age.

TRY THIS The Chicago Quadrilateral summarizes the basics of Anglican identity this way:

- We shape our prayers after a common form.
- We live in relationship facilitated by our bishops, and connected to the Church of England.
- We return to the Holy Scriptures as the source of our wisdom and life.
- We offer the sacraments of Baptism and Communion.

Gather with a group and identify additional local expressions of the Episcopal identity, especially the ones that matter most to you.

Chapter 8

Secularism and a Thoughtful yet Mystical Church

If globalization and its cousin, pluralism (defined as a situation in which people of different social classes, religions, races, etc., function together in a society but continue to have their different traditions and interests), have introduced new cultures and faith traditions into American life, they have also paved the way for another choice: secularism, or no religion at all.

The Pew Center has been tracing this shift and says the number of Americans who do not identify with any religion—known as "Nones"—now stands at one-fifth of the U.S. public and a third of adults under 30.[27] If the trend continues, and there is no reason to think it will not, more than half of America will identify as a None in 2042.[28]

There is a nuance in these statistics that may surprise people of faith: these Nones believe in God (68 percent), think of themselves

---

27. Pew Religion and Public Life Project, "'Nones' on the Rise." http://www.pewforum.org/2012/10/09/nones-on-the-rise, October 9, 2012.

28. American Religious Identification Survey (ARIS), 2001, prog.trincoll.edu/ISSSC/DataArchive/index.asp, as cited in Butler Bass, Christianity After Religion, 46.

secularism: the rejection, indifference, or exclusion of religion and religious considerations

as spiritual but not religious (37 percent), and even pray every day (21 percent).[29] They just do not see what that has to do with a formal religious community.

Christian decline is one thing. Another tectonic shift is the strength of public resistance to Christianity and other organized religions, or secularism (rejection, indifference or exclusion of religion and religious considerations). Even fifteen years ago, you would have been hard-pressed to find a best seller making the case for atheism. Now the "new atheists" like Christopher Hitchens and Richard Dawkins aren't so new at all—instead, these titles regularly post on best-seller lists. Atheists are forming their own communities and student organizations; a friend of Stephanie's recently served as the atheist chaplain at Harvard University.

What happened? Robert Putnam and David Campbell trace the development in their book *American Grace: How Religion Divides and Unites Us*, and they come to some clear conclusions. For instance, they note:

> A growing number of Americans, especially young people, have come to disavow religion. For many, their aversion is unease with the association between religion and conservative politics. If religion equals Republican, then they have decided religion is not for them. [30]

The Barna Group did its own study of emerging generations, and the results are troubling for Christians across the ideological spectrum. It turns out that very few young people want to be associated with "those Christians." One 29-year-old they interviewed admitted his true feelings about religion: "Christianity seems like

---

29. "'Nones' on the Rise."

30. Robert D. Putnam and David E. Campbell, *American Grace: How Religion Divides and Unites Us* (New York: Simon and Schuster, 2010), 3.

an old, broken-down building that I have to drive by every day. I don't even notice it anymore."[31]

The secular wave is also crashing on another shore. Europeans can chart the drop in church attendance just as levels of education, industrialization and general prosperity rise. And while America has resisted that trend and remained something of a City on a Hill, it seems the wave just took a bit longer to arrive. Now, it is here.

The American Way?

The secularization of American life is not a sign of some great evil at work. It may be a return to another great American impulse: freedom. The founders might not have expected their commitment to religious freedom would result in some people having no religion at all, but there is something quintessentially American about being able to forge your own destiny. We do not believe in coercion, and ours is one of the few industrialized cultures where social mobility is a norm.

In other words, just because your parents were middle class, that does not mean you cannot become upper (or lower) class. You might have grown up in the South, but if you move to Los Angeles and reinvent yourself, you are simply living the American dream. And even if you grew up in a strict Roman Catholic or evangelical household, you deserve the freedom to ask big questions, entertain doubts, and eventually find your true path.

How many Baby Boomers and members of the Silent Generation were only pretending to have a faith they did not feel, going to church because it was the way to get or keep your job, make friends in your neighborhood, and provide moral teachings for your children? Increasing religious freedom—even the free-

---

31. David Kinnaman and Gabe Lyons, *unChristian: What a New Generation Really Thinks about Christianity . . . and Why It Matters* (Grand Rapids, MI: Baker Books, 2008), 74.

dom to not have a religion—seems the natural result of living the American Way.

So Alone

A highly educated, scientifically sophisticated society seems destined to bend toward secularism. Where does that leave us? Stephanie spent most of her youth as an avowed agnostic. She recalls coming to school on Monday and having to fend off friends who had prayed for her in their youth groups on a Sunday. They were eager to give her reason #32 why she needed to become a Christian. What her friends didn't understand was that Christianity didn't make sense to her, and she wasn't going to adopt any belief that didn't jibe intellectually.

Road Rule 10 Instead of focusing on getting to the right answer (which often implies a judgment), focus on asking the right questions. Pose questions that explore the subject, broaden the perspectives, and move the conversation deeper to achieve mutual understanding.

How did she move from agnosticism to priesthood? Science and philosophy made lots of sense, but the universe still held mysteries, and they haunted her. Like other human beings and most Americans, she was still deeply spiritual. She also found life without God was just plain lonely. She wanted a container for her questions and dreams, a way to name the inescapable sense that a love "out there" encompassed everything. Quantum physics spoke of quarks and leaps and unifying theories—none of which anyone could actually see. Why could she not have God, especially in Jesus, with whom she could be in life-changing relationship?

For many of us, the secular life has a certain reasonable integrity, but it also feels rigid, small, and lonely. And in the end, we wonder if perhaps there is a truth beyond the one that can be named and proven. We just wish there was a way to be both reasonable and faithful.

Reason Meets Faith

We have spoken in earlier chapters of the three-legged stool of Anglicanism, and the fact that Episcopalians answer our big questions using three sources in conversation with each other: the Holy Bible, the church's traditions, and human reason. That trust in reason—which has its own shadow side, as we will explore in Part III—means this church may be well equipped to engage a pluralistic, secular culture in meaningful dialogue.

How many currently secular people think they would have to release their belief in gender equality or science in order to be religious? Eric was invited to preach at a church in a high-tech area. Word got out that he used to be an engineer and many came to hear him. Knowing his likely audience, Eric prepared a sermon that consciously engaged the dialogue between Christian faith and science. For instance, the Trinity became the basic building blocks of our faith, just as 1s and 0s are the basic building blocks of the digital world.

During coffee hour, the scientists and engineers in the community greeted Eric like a rock star. "Thank you so much," one of them said. "This is the first time I've heard thermocouple mentioned in a sermon, and it made sense."

The Episcopal Way celebrates asking questions and engaging in dialogue, even in areas where religion has not traditionally been comfortable, even when there may be no clear answer at the end. The goal is to listen for God's voice as we explore a complex and pluralistic world where new information and perspectives are constantly emerging.

The early followers of Jesus engaged in the very same dialogue. In the tenth chapter of the book of Acts, the apostle Peter struggled because God told him to go beyond the circle of the Jews and welcome gentiles into the Christian community. He could not imagine how it made sense: they were not circumcised, they had not learned the ancient stories of the Hebrew people—how could they become Christian?

Peter did not know what the outcome might be, but he responded to God's call to go out and meet a gentile named Cornelius. To his surprise, he met a man who loved God and cared for his neighbors as well as any Christian. Peter was thoughtful, flexible, and humble, and as a result he was changed. "I truly understand that God shows no partiality, but in every nation anyone who fears him and does what is right is acceptable to him" (Acts 10:34–35). This story captures the journey we take on the Episcopal Way: we trust that God is still revealing the truth, and we keep asking questions, examining what we observe and comparing it to the traditions we have received, until that truth comes into sharper view.

Bow to the Mystery

The Episcopal Way is gifted for asking questions, incorporating reason, and being willing to change when God reveals a new truth before our very eyes. Another blessing we offer in a hyper-reasonable, secular culture is the ability to know when it is time to stop talking. In other words, when to bow in awe and let mystery be mystery.

Stephanie spent seven years working at St. Paul's Cathedral in downtown Boston. The huge building was simply decorated, to the point that some people wondered whether it was a church. But day after day, people walked in—downtown workers on lunch break, tourists wandering Boston Common, homeless people seeking warmth and peace. Each entered the church and looked around in awe and wonder, feeling the sense of scale and realizing this beauty was at once created by humans but not just for humans. Most of us have sensed the same thing in a house of worship: that hushed, awe-filled, "wow" feeling.

Episcopalians are comfortable with that sense of awe, wonder, and not-knowing (or just not needing to know). We have incorporated it into our theology. We are not likely to get wrapped up in questions like, "How did the communion bread become Jesus' flesh, and the wine become Jesus' blood?" Richard Hooker, one of the first Anglican theologians, simply responded:

> "This heavenly food is given for the satisfying of our empty souls, not for the exercising of our curious and subtle wits. Why should any cogitation possess the mind of a faithful communicant but this: O my God, thou art true, O my soul thou art happy?"[32]

Like Hooker, a faithful Episcopalian might answer: "I only need to know that, whenever I receive this bread and wine, I become more and more part of the mystical body of Jesus. His life is inside mine, because of that bread and wine. It is his body and blood."

The Episcopal Way glories in mysteries like these, and often puts them to poetry—the original language of mystery, where silences between the words often speak louder than the words themselves. George Herbert, a sixteenth-century priest and poet, wrote this poem to capture his own experience of intimate relation with God. (This text has been set to music and sung for centuries.)

"The Call"
Come, my Way, my Truth, my Life:
Such a way as gives us breath;
Such a truth as ends all strife,
Such a life as killeth death.

Come, my Light, my Feast, my Strength:
Such a light as shows a feast,
Such a feast as mends in length,
Such a strength as makes his guest.

---

32. Richard Hooker, *Of the Laws of Ecclesiastical Polity,* as cited in Schmidt, *Glorious Companions,* 31.

Come, my Joy, my Love, my Heart:
Such a joy as none can move,
Such a love as none can part,
Such a heart as joys in love.

How do we enter into this union with God? How does God decide who to love? How does life "killeth death"? What matters to George Herbert is receiving the gift of union, love, and new life that God has offered. We can open to receive these mysteries without having to create a diagram explaining precisely how they came to be. There's a relief in not having to figure it all out. There is a freedom in using and appreciating reason but also knowing its limits.

Not everyone needs a reasonable yet mysterious church, but plenty of people living in a secular culture might like to be in conversation with one. Some of us need help bringing reason into conversation with faith. Some of us need to turn off our brains and just feel. The Episcopal Way is roomy enough to accommodate both impulses, even if they show up in the same person.

TRY THIS Describe an authentic spiritual or mystical experience: a moment when you tapped into a divine, transcendent reality.

- How old were you?
- Where were you?
- Do you recall sounds or images, feelings or smells?
- Who was with you?
- Why do you think it was "spiritual"?

Try this exercise with a group of friends and invite each person to share. At the end, talk about the common elements in the stories.

PART III

The World Meets a Changing Church

So much has changed in our nation and world in the last twenty years, and there is plenty that Christians in the Episcopal Church can share to heal and embrace these changing landscapes. The reverse is also true: there are patterns and practices in the church's life that once made sense, but now present potential barriers to relationship with the cultures and communities where we live.

These points of disconnect are not inherent failures; they are actually opportunities. Can we adapt and reclaim the heart of Christian identity shaped by the Episcopal Way? Can we listen to the wisdom of our neighbors and develop relationships that heal and bless us equally?

Just as Part II studied the fundamental paradigm shifts that have shaped life in the twenty-first century, and the blessings and shadows in each, in this section we will explore some of the fundamental marks of the Episcopal Way, their light and shadow, and the way the world's wisdom may help to redeem the church and return us to the Way.

Road Rule 11 Always discover and affirm the goodness and gifts of a community first. After you have laid this foundation, the discussion of issues and problems is much more productive and constructive.

The Book of Revelation provides some provocative images and language for a conversation like this. In it, John has a vision of Christ addressing the angels of the seven churches in the form of letters like this:

> To the angel of the church in Ephesus . . . I know your works, your toil and your patient endurance. . . . But I have this against you, that you have abandoned the love you had at first. Remember then from what you have fallen; repent, and do the works you did at first. (Revelation 2:1–2, 4–5)

Walter Wink's commentary on these letters breaks the code wide open. He notices, for instance, that Jesus is not pointing an angry finger at the people of the churches. He calls out "the angel." What is this angel? Wink says it "seemed to be the corporate personality of the church, its ethos or spirit or essence."[33] He imagines that every church has an angel like this.

The angel is something like the DNA of a church. It is also "the bearer of that institution's divine vocation"—that is, the angel represents the hope for what the church (or institution) was supposed to be, if it were living in tune with the dream of God. When a church turns away from that divine vocation, Wink says, it becomes "demonic" or fallen. That sounds incredibly harsh, but for Wink, the prescription is not to then cast out the demon. Rather, we hear Jesus calling the fallen angel back to its divine task.[34]

---

33. Walter Wink, *The Powers That Be: Theology for a New Millennium* (New York: Doubleday, 1998), 3–4.

34. Ibid., 24.

That is what Christ is doing in Revelation: praising the angels of the churches for their good work, pointing out how that goodness has turned, and then offering a path for the fallen angel to return to its divine calling.

If we think of the Episcopal Way as the angel of the church—its DNA, its essence—what would the divine voice say to this angel today? What would it praise? Where has it fallen as it has sought to fulfill the divine call? And what path for redemption would that divine voice give the church? The chapters in this section aim to address some of those challenges and opportunities.

The Episcopal Way	The Fall	The Redemption
Adaptive	Fearful of change	Return to Via Media and reform tradition
Beautiful	Idolatrous and rigid	Practice justice and seek Christ in others
Generous	Elitist	Practice mutual giving and receiving with our neighbors
Reasonable	Ambivalent about God	Fall in love with God

In our changing world, Episcopalians are often bewildered and confused about how to be faithful to our call. We know we can be flexible and adaptive in the face of major change, but we also get trapped by fear of change. Our love of beauty draws us closer to God, but it can also make us sound like culturally narrow dictators. We have held great privilege as a church, and that has blinded us to the gifts of groups with less privilege. And our great capacity for reason has enabled us to sometimes think our way out of relationship with God.

Some of us feel guilty. Some of us want to scrap the whole enterprise. Some of us feel hopeless. Some of us are so fearful that we do not remember our original call. Thankfully, the Episcopal Way itself holds the key: do not be tempted by the extremes. Name the community's blessing and goodness. Be courageous and honest about our fallenness. Then look around—at the world and at the ancient pathways—and seek a middle path of redemption and new life as the people of God today.

TRY THIS Complete the following letter for the congregation or ministry to which you are most closely linked:

To the angel of _____ (name of your congregation/ministry) _____ ,

I know your works: ____ (name the blessings and good works) ____ ,

But I say this to you: _____ (name the fallenness) _____ ,

And I call you to repent: ____ (name the process for redemption) ____ .

Chapter 9

Returning to the Via Media

On July 29, 1974, eleven women were ordained to the priesthood in Philadelphia. Even though they were not the first in the Anglican Communion (the first was Rev. Florence Li Tim-Oi, ordained in 1944 in Hong Kong), they were the ones who broke the American church's "tradition."

On August 15, 1974, the House of Bishops called an emergency meeting, denounced the ordinations, and declared them invalid. Although there were no rules specifically prohibiting women's ordination to the priesthood, charges were filed against the bishops who ordained the women and attempts were made to prevent the women from serving their priestly ministries.

By September 1976, after countless conversations, hearings, and prayers, the General Convention of the Episcopal Church approved the ordination of women to the priesthood *and* episcopate.

Eric was in college during this time, and he remembers the rollercoaster ride. On one end of the spectrum were those who believed the church had taken a leap toward the dream of God. Others were terrified of the change and believed they had lost their church. They worried about the impact on biblical interpretation (Scripture), the Episcopal Church's relationship with the Roman

Catholic and Orthodox Church (Tradition), and whether women were truly equipped for priestly authority (Reason). Could the church change like this and still be the church?

In 1989, the Diocese of Massachusetts elected the Right Reverend Barbara Harris as the first woman bishop in the Anglican Communion. In 2006, we elected Bishop Katharine Jefferts Schori as Presiding Bishop, making her the first woman primate (or head of a province or national church) in the Anglican Communion. As this book went to print, women made up a sizeable portion of the students in Episcopal seminaries. Today, it is fair to say that women priests and bishops—once the source of severe division—are an essential part of the life of the Episcopal Church. They are part of our tradition.

A Reform Tradition

Tradition is not a set of static values, beliefs, rules, and structures. Even when we use the phrase "traditional values," we are referring to something that was once upon a time new, and over time became part of the tradition. In that sense, tradition can be thought of as a verb—we are constantly "traditioning."

This notion makes perfect sense for a church long referred to as the Protestant Episcopal Church in the United States of America. Until 1964, it was the only name in use. Being Protestant means we are a church born during the Reformation; it names our commitment to always be reforming. The word "Episcopal" in the title points to our roots in ancient, catholic forms that emphasize the leadership of a bishop and common prayer. We are traditional, but the traditioning process goes on.

The process is apparent if you take a look at the 1979 Book of Common Prayer and *The Hymnal 1982*. For most Episcopalians today these are the traditional books. However, during the 1970s and 1980s, the material in these books inspired heated debates.

Many Episcopalians believed the 1928 Prayer Book was the finest liturgical resource created, and the closest to the seventeenth-century prayers that made their hearts sing. Few then could have imagined these books would be seen as "traditional" and even in need of renewal within a generation.

More recently, the ordination of openly gay priests (beginning with Reverend Ellen Barrett in 1977) and bishops (beginning with the Right Reverend Gene Robinson) represented a sharp break with tradition. Through our church's comprehensive decision-making process, deep ongoing conversation, and commitment to communion, we have worked through controversy and arrived at consensus on matters that once flew in the face of tradition. And so the ongoing process of reformation continues.

TRY THIS Recall a moment when you saw a faith community go through a change.

- What was the process?
- How did the members explore the issues?
- How was the decision made?
- How did the community navigate the change, especially if some members did not support it?
- How do people feel about the change today? Is it still a sore spot or an accepted "tradition"?

When Tradition Freezes

On the one hand, the Episcopal Church is actively engaged in traditioning to meet shifting cultural realities. There is another side to our identity: "The Frozen Chosen." Sometimes the title gets tossed out as a joke; other times, it's clearly an indictment. Is it truth?

It is, insofar as we have fallen short of our calling to keep actively traditioning rather than becoming protectors of The Tradition.

The moment we stop traditioning and refuse to let go of the things with which we are familiar, we become frozen, unable to dialogue with a changing world and unwilling to revisit our understanding of scriptures and traditions anew. We become unfaithful.

Some Episcopalians are frozen in the 1950s. They remember the church's glory days, when the pews were full, Sunday school was packed, and female volunteers kept the church's ministries humming. The church communities formed in that Christianity-affirming context were good and faithful. They make sense in very few of our contemporary contexts.

Some are frozen in the 1970s—focused on a church building, fixed on the priest as caregiver, glued to the Prayer Book and Hymnal, even though more recent resources have been authorized for church use (and even more non-book-based resources have emerged). That way of ministry was a faithful response for church people at the time. However, the world has moved on. Jesus invites us to minister in new contexts. Will the church move, as well?

Road Rule 12 When you find yourself thinking "We have always done it this way" and dismissing an idea, stop and recall that this "way" was new at one point. What was its original purpose? Is it still applicable? Discuss the question with others, especially some who know the background and current context.

Reclaiming the Via Media

The Hebrew word for truth, *emet,* is composed of three letters—א (*alef*), מ (*mem*), and ת (*tav*)—the first, middle, and last letters of the Hebrew alphabet. In order to discern the truth, one must know the beginning, the middle, and the end. For those walking the Episcopal Way, this means we must take into account the beginning of our faith story (Scripture), the intervening two thousand or more years that Christians have lived the story (Tradition), and everything we can observe in this present moment and piece together about the future (Reason).

If this sounds like the Via Media, the first principle of the Episcopal Way we discussed in the Introduction, it is. Another word for this complex way of walking with Jesus and each other is "comprehensive." In 1968 the Lambeth Conference, the every-ten-years meeting of bishops from across the worldwide Anglican Communion, issued a statement that describes the concept well:

Comprehensiveness demands agreement on fundamentals, while tolerating disagreement on matters in which Christians may differ without feeling the necessity of breaking communion. In the mind of an Anglican, comprehensiveness is not compromise. Nor is it to bargain one truth for another. It is not a sophisticated word for syncretism. Rather it implies that the apprehension of truth is a growing thing; we only gradually succeed in "knowing the truth." For we believe that in leading us into the truth the Holy Spirit may have some surprises in store for us in the future as he has had in the past.

What has this kind of comprehensiveness looked like on the ground? Priest and scholar William Porcher Dubose embodied it with heartbreaking clarity. A son of the Confederacy, he grew up in South Carolina, fought for the Rebel cause in the Civil War, and argued to protect the institution of slavery. When he came home from the battlefield, his parents were dead and General William T. Sherman had burned the Dubose family home on his devastating march to the sea.

Dubose had every reason to turn bitter and cling to his old convictions. Instead, he opened out and began to understand that God might just be revealing truths more complex than any one side could possibly grasp. He insisted that he had to be part of

comprehensiveness: a broad position that gathers multiple perspectives to discern the whole truth, and accommodates agreement on fundamentals and disagreement on particulars

a truly catholic (universal) church, because nothing less than "the mind of the church as a whole, could be broad enough and comprehensive enough to embrace at once on all its sides the totality of the truth of Jesus Christ."[35] One person cannot have a lock on the wisdom of God, but if I combine my partial truth with yours, and if we create enough space for still more approaches and perspectives, then we will surely get closer to what God intends.

Comprehensiveness like this is hard to find in our contemporary contexts. In an age of gridlocked government and political positioning, it would be refreshing to see a church break out of the either/or paradigm. If we did, we would find plenty of allies in emerging generations. Thanks to the pluralism we spoke of earlier, these younger Americans have a higher tolerance for ambiguity than past generations. A single, unchanging answer or a frozen tradition simply will not satisfy.

The Episcopal Church can repent of our frozenness and reclaim the gifts of Via Media, reformation traditions and comprehensiveness. We can become a gracious community where people listen for multiple perspectives, explore and discern the truth, and adapt traditions so they speak faithfully in this day. We can celebrate the difficult, messy, always unfolding path that is the Episcopal Way.

TRY THIS When gathering with others to discuss concerns and issues, present a set of Respectful Communication Guidelines similar to the ones that follow and invite participants to uphold them.[36]

R = take RESPONSIBILITY for what you say and feel without blaming others

35. Robert Boak Slocum, *The Theology of William Porcher Dubose: Life, Movement, and Being* (Columbia, SC: University of South Carolina Press, 2000), 95.

36. See Eric H. F. Law, *The Bush Was Blazing But Not Consumed* (St. Louis, MO: Chalice Press, 1996), 87.

E = use EMPATHETIC listening

S = be SENSITIVE to differences in communication styles

P = PONDER what you hear and feel before you speak

E = EXAMINE your own assumptions and perceptions

C = keep CONFIDENTIALITY

T = TRUST ambiguity because we are NOT here to debate
who is right or wrong

Chapter 10

Uniting Beauty and Justice

"Worship the Lord in the beauty of holiness: Come let us adore him."

The "beauty of holiness" echoes through the Psalms (29, 96, and 110). It also reverberates through Episcopal worship. And even if you never saw or heard the words, walking into an Episcopal Church proves it: the cascading light, the stained glass, the icons, the tapestries, the vestments, the choral anthems, the grand organ, the flow of worship and painstaking attention to detail.

Episcopalians do not just have "good taste." We understand beauty to be intimately connected to holiness, a doorway we step through in order to be transported beyond ourselves and into the very presence of God.

Before she was Episcopalian or even Christian, Stephanie remembers being moved by the poetry of English luminaries like William Wordsworth and George Herbert. In her sophomore year of high school, she had to memorize John Donne's "Meditation 17" and recite it in front of her class. Halfway through, at these lines, she started to cry:

No man is an island, entire of itself; every man is a piece of the continent, a part of the main. If a clod be washed away by the sea, Europe is the less, as well as if a promontory were, as well as if a manor of thy friend's or of thine own were: any man's death diminishes me, because I am involved in mankind, and therefore never send to know for whom the bell tolls; it tolls for thee.

At the time, she did not know all these poets were Anglicans, or that two of them (George Herbert and John Donne) were priests. She did not know C. S. Lewis, Madeleine L'Engle, and even Desmond Tutu—who led the faithful of South Africa with his clear and beautiful vision of the dream of God—were all Anglicans. She could not have guessed that this church—a church that spoke of faith not only in didactic prose but in sumptuous poetry—would someday be her first true Christian home. Beauty brought her home to God.

The arts have been part of Christian experience and devotion for as long as there have been Christians. It began with the first followers of Jesus telling and retelling stories. Drawings depicting symbols and images essential to the sharing of faith stories were etched on the walls of secret places where Christians met.

As Christianity gained wider acceptance in Europe, artists—painters, sculptors, architects, stained-glass window makers, composers—were employed to create magnificent offerings to embody the faith story. Since most people did not know how to read, arts were the principal media for people to learn about their faith.

During the Protestant Reformation, when reformers took back the Bible and placed it in the hands of the people, there was a backlash against art. Puritan church leaders in England and in the United States were suspicious of anything that looked "Catholic," so they tore out statues, shattered stained glass windows, housed animals in the area where the altar stood, and offered the Eucharist only every few months (and even then with only a minimum of ceremony).[37]

---

37. John Orens, "The Anglo-Catholic Vision," Duquesne Center for Incarnational Social Thought (Pittsburgh, PA: Duquesne University), 4. Available at http://www.duq.edu/Documents/philosophy/_pdf/The%20Anglo-Catholic%20 Vision.pdf

Anglo-Catholic:
accents the catholic side of Anglican identity, including sacraments, the authority of clergy, and beautiful, formal liturgy

By the nineteenth century, a group of young English clergy were determined to reclaim the Catholic side of the Anglican tradition. Originally known as the Oxford Movement (the young men were based in Oxford, England), the movement reclaimed beauty, sacraments, and historic Catholic traditions as a vehicle for entering relationship with God. As these priests moved into depressed neighborhoods and started new churches, they celebrated stunning images, poetry, architecture, and liturgical practices that proclaimed God's presence in places the rest of the world had written off as useless.

Their impact continues to resonate through much of the Episcopal Church today, often under the rubric of Anglo-Catholicism. St. Paul's Episcopal Church in Seattle, a progressive Anglo-Catholic parish, explains this tradition well on its website:

> We are drawn to liturgy that emphasizes adoration. We enter into this adoration through listening to and singing beautiful music, chanting, the use of gesture and embodied prayer (genuflection, bowing, crossing oneself) and the engagement of the senses (incense, baptismal water, bells, beautiful vestments, etc.). As Anglo-Catholics, our ultimate worship experience is one in which we not only glimpse but enter into and taste something of the beauty and mystery of God.

Anglo-Catholicism is now deeply embedded in the Episcopal Way. Just walk into almost any Episcopal cathedral and pretend that you do not know how to read; you will experience the story of God's movement in human history as told through the other senses—sights, sounds, smells, touch.

Dostoyevsky once wrote, "The world will be saved by beauty." Anglicans such as Madeleine L'Engle would tell you that beauty will save our souls. "We do not draw people to Christ by loudly discrediting what they believe, by telling them how wrong they are and how right we are, but by showing them a light that is so lovely that they want with all their hearts to know the source of it."[38]

Squeezing Out the Spirit

Of course, the pendulum will swing. Too much emphasis on words and rationalism, and the beauty of God disappears. But if there is too much emphasis on the beautiful, we may grow obsessed with the things we have created for God and mistake them for the actual life of God. They become idols. This anonymous poem from the nineteenth century sums up the story of such excesses in the liturgy:

One by one, Innovations came in due course
High Altars, bright brasses, great candles in force,
Uplifting of arms most decidedly high,
Turning backs on the people as if they were shy.
There were chasubles white with the sign of the yoke,
Albs, copes, capes, birettas, and volumes of smoke.[39]

The poem recalls the introduction of more and more grand liturgical accoutrement: worship filled with "volumes of smoke" and vestments galore (albs, copes, capes, birettas)—less for the sake of God and more for our own elevation. In our deep love for God and the things that have communicated God's love, followers of the Episcopal Way can also get caught in obsessive attention to detail and doing things the "proper" way. That rigidity can leave little room for the grace and surprising movement of God, or for other cultures' images of the holy.

38. Madeleine L'Engle, *Walking on Water: Reflections on Faith and Art* (New York: North Point Press, 1995), 122.

39. Anonymous, cited in John Orens, *Stewart Headlam's Radical Anglicanism: The Mass, The Masses, and the Music Hall* (Champaign, IL: University of Illinois Press, 2003), 7.

A church on this path will be far from incarnational. It would need to return to the Episcopal Way.

Road Rule 13 When you find yourself drawn to an extreme of any practice or belief, step back and ask: what other sources do I need to consult to maintain a balanced spiritual life? Practicing the Episcopal Way does not mean we lack conviction; it means our convictions emerge from a balanced and gracious process of discernment.

The Beauty of Jesus

Where is redemption, when a church is tempted to love itself more than it loves God or its neighbors? We would suggest a return to the most beautiful part of the Christian faith and the Episcopal Way: the love of Jesus and his love for the world.

People who have nothing to do with Christianity admire Jesus. Mahatma Gandhi reportedly told a Christian missionary: "Oh, I don't reject your Christ. I love your Christ. It is just that so many of you Christians are so unlike your Christ." He wanted to see Christians giving their lives in love for God and God's world, as Jesus did. Lots of non-Christians—and plenty of non-practicing Christians—would say the same. They are quick to quote back to us, "Jesus said, 'Love God and love your neighbor as yourself'" (paraphrase, Mark 12:30–31). They have an intuitive sense that we cannot love God, whom we have not seen, if we do not love our neighbors, who are right in front of us (1 John 4:20). And they are right.

The Oxford priests who brought the Catholic spirit back to Anglicanism understood all of this. They knew that you cannot separate loving the body of Jesus, in the sacrament of bread and wine, and loving the body of Jesus, in the sacrament of our neighbors. Edward Pusey preached that God intends poor people to be "the visible representatives to the rich of his Only Begotten Son, who, being rich, for us men and our salvation, became poor, who, in their earthly lot, exalted our human nature to the union with his divine. . . ." Pusey was horrified by churches that decorate the walls with pictures of Jesus, "while man, the image of God and representative of Christ, [we] clothe not. . . ."[40]

Anglo-Catholic priests like Pusey often presided over gorgeous churches with transcendent liturgies, but they did it in depressed and forsaken urban areas, to provide a vision of God's beauty and love in the midst of pain. How can the beauty of holiness serve the same purpose today? How will love for God's beauty translate into love for God's most beautiful creation, made in God's own image? How will the heavenly banquet we taste at communion feed and strengthen people to join God's movement in the world?

Worship at most Episcopal churches ends with a deacon calling out, "Let us go forth to love and serve the Lord. Alleluia." Others close with, "The mass has ended. Our service now begins." In either case, the people respond, "Thanks be to God. Alleluia!" With those words, we affirm two deep truths: Glorious churches and carefully orchestrated liturgies are faithful offerings to God, and they facilitate our journey closer to God's own heart. They are also a powerful force pushing us out to love and serve the Lord. Alleluia.

TRY THIS The next time you participate in an Episcopal worship service, consciously make connections between the insights and inspiration you receive and the needs and concerns you observe in your neighborhood, town, or city. How would you concretely respond to the deacon's call, "Let us go forth to love and serve the Lord"?

40. Orens, "The Anglo-Catholic Vision," 10.

Chapter 11

Practicing Mutuality with the Other

America has no national or state church. No Lutheran Church, like the Germans and Scandinavians. No Roman Catholic Church, like Italy. No Church of England, like England.

America has no national church, but the Episcopal Church has often functioned as one. We built Washington National Cathedral, the massive gothic cathedral on a hill overlooking the nation's capital. Closer to the center of the action, St. John's Episcopal Church in Lafayette Square has hosted the President's inauguration day prayer service for about half of the last twenty administrations.

Before independence, we were the church of the colonial governing class. After independence, we remained the church of the governing and owning class. Thankfully, we have often borne that responsibility with grace. When communities needed churches, schools, or hospitals here in America and in far-flung nations, we have built them. Trinity Church-Wall Street in New York City used its billions, in part, to fund the effort to shatter apartheid in South Africa. To this day, when soup kitchens and homeless shelters and countless social services need a home, we open the doors of our churches and welcome them into our midst, often without charge.

It is all a part of living a gospel-focused life, as shaped by Jesus himself. He asked everyone to be generous and faithful. He encouraged the poor, when he told the story of the widow who gave her last two coins out of pure faith (Luke 21:1–4). He also encouraged those with lots of resources to share and to experience the freedom of releasing their privilege.

Clearly, some people with means took him up on the offer. Recall Lydia, whose generosity made the ministry of the early church possible:

> On the Sabbath day we went outside the gate by the river, where we supposed there was a place of prayer; and we sat down and spoke to the women who had gathered there. A certain woman named Lydia, a worshiper of God, was listening to us; she was from the city of Thyatira and a dealer in purple cloth. The Lord opened her heart to listen eagerly to what was said by Paul. When she and her household were baptized, she urged us, saying, "If you have judged me to be faithful to the Lord, come and stay at my home." And she prevailed upon us. (Acts 16:13–15)

Lydia was not alone. From the beginning of Jesus' ministry until the end, people of means sacrificed for the sake of the mission of God. Jesus gathered and loved centurions, tax collectors, prostitutes—any number of people with economic privilege. He was less concerned with judgment and punishment; he welcomed them to join a kingdom-shaped community, share what they had, stop participating in oppressive or exploitative systems, and become reconciled with God and their neighbors. The privileged have a place in the kingdom, and they certainly have a place in the Episcopal Church.

With Great Privilege . . .

The story of Episcopal privilege and status is well known to many Americans. In 1978, journalists Kit and Frederica Konolige wrote a 600-page social history titled *The Power of Their Glory: America's Ruling Class: The Episcopalians*. The Konoliges had little interest in religion; they conducted their exhaustive study because they saw the Episcopal Church as the institution that embodies and protects the culture of America's ruling class, welcoming hand-selected outsiders to join our rarefied ranks.

> These are the people we have called the Episcocrats. . . . What has made them so important to the country is that their set of attitudes and mores, fertilized by a distinctly Anglophiliac and Episcopal atmosphere of feeling, has been adopted by non-Episcopalians as the standard for upper-class conduct (in law, government, and business). The influence of the distinctly Episcopalian institutions—the prep schools, the men's colleges, and the metropolitan clubs—can hardly be overstated.[41]

Religious life in America has changed quite a lot, and so has the cultural landscape. But one could argue that the "Episcocracy" is alive and well within our church's life. We have not successfully embraced the blessings of people on the margins. We have not exposed our need and vulnerability to a world with plenty to teach and give us.

The simplest reason is not only class or race related. It comes down to love. We all love what has been holy in our eyes, and expect it will enlighten and warm others' hearts as it has ours. Eric and Stephanie have both heard Episcopalians speak this earnest hope. "These traditions have represented God to me," people say with deep affection. "My greatest prayer is that they will be equally transformative and beautiful to others. If not, I hope they will find a church they can love the way I love this one."

While our intentions are good, the results may not be. Gathering people with similar preferences and experiences can produce a one-dimensional, static community. As of 2008, nearly 80 percent of Episcopalians had attended college or even earned graduate de-

---

41. Kit and Frederica Konolige, *The Power of Their Glory: America's Ruling Class: The Episcopalians* (New York: Simon and Schuster, 1978), 29.

grees, the highest proportion of educated people of any church in America.[42] Meanwhile, 35 percent of Episcopal adults made more than $100,000 a year, the highest proportion of wealthy people of any church in America.[43]

The statistics speak: we function as the church of the elite, a group drawn by common aesthetics and culture, with a few inside and many more outside. We must pray for redemption.

The Grace of Giving

There is no hiding from privilege, and there is no removing it from human society, this side of heaven. The only realistic question is, How will you use it? The Episcopal Church could become a powerful witness for the gospel of Jesus if it acknowledged the richness of its heritage and its continued privilege in the United States, and *then* responded to its neighbors with humility, curiosity, and generosity.

We may not have the privilege we once claimed—certainly, not every Episcopalian is wealthy or highly privileged. But as a whole church we have plenty of gifts, especially for a denomination that makes up less than one-half of 1 percent of the American population. Imagine the power we could unleash if we were more like Lydia, willing to convert and offer our resources to nourish mission and ministry.

Road Rule 14 If you feel guilty about having more than others, transform that guilt into an opportunity. Learn what systems have made it possible for you to have much while others have little. Figure out ways to share your resources and talent, and appreciate the resources and talent of others you might not have respected before.

42. *U.S. Religious Landscape Survey: Religious Affiliation, Diverse and Dynamic* (Washington, DC: Pew Research Center, 2008), 85.
43. Ibid., 79.

Following Jesus' invitation this way is never as easy as it sounds. Remember the rich young ruler in the Gospel of Luke. He knew the faith by heart, so Jesus gave him one more challenge: "Sell all that you own and distribute the money to the poor, and you will have treasure in heaven; then come, follow me." When he heard Jesus' words, the young man was sad because he had lots of money and lots to lose. Jesus acknowledged the truth: "How hard it is for those who have wealth to enter the kingdom of God!" (Luke 18:18–24).

Jesus wasn't punishing the young man. He was giving him the key to new life: share your power, share your resources, allow yourself to need others, and you will be truly free. In God's kingdom, there is a faithful exchange of power and resources. The rich let go and receive blessings they never imagined. The poor open and discover they have gifts and resources beyond measure. That's what the kingdom looks like, and what churches should model.

The Grace of Receiving

The Episcopal Church could learn plenty about the grace of giving *and* of receiving. Jesus' earliest disciples had to learn to be vulnerable and generous in the communities they entered; that's why Jesus sent them out with these words:

> Go on your way. . . . Carry no purse, no bag, no sandals; and greet no one on the road. Whatever house you enter, first say, "Peace to this house!" And if anyone is there who shares in peace, your peace will rest on that person; but if not, it will return to you. Remain in the same house, eating and drinking whatever they provide, for the laborer deserves to be paid. Do not move about from house to house. Whenever you enter a town and its people welcome you, eat what is set before you; cure the sick who are there, and say to them, "The kingdom of God has come near to you." (Luke 10:3–9)

And so they went, not with their hands full, like benefactors ready to give from their bounty, but with empty hands and pockets, with plenty of room to receive. They were ready to weave the gifts of the good news of Jesus Christ together with the gifts of the culture around them. If they saw people who were willing to partner for God's mission, they were supposed to come alongside and share peace with them. No one expected the church to be the dominant force.

Clearly, the America we now inhabit has more in common with that early environment than with the privileged status we have enjoyed for several centuries. The kind of deep listening, humble presence, and generosity Jesus' followers practiced is precisely what is called for in this changing world. Listen to the poor, the struggling middle class, or anyone who lacks your privilege and power in a particular area. Listen, receive the gift of the margins, and Jesus will turn your heart of stone into a heart of flesh.

Elitism may be embedded in the history of the Episcopal Church, and it may shape much of our present, but it need not be our future. Stephanie has spent years studying churches that have charted this new course. She calls them "radically welcoming": congregations that actively welcome newcomers and the marginalized to bring their voices, gifts, power, and presence into the heart of the church, where they can truly shape the church's ministry, leadership, and worship. The guiding principle for radical welcome is mutual transformation, or as one leader put it: "You change us, we change you."

At the Cathedral in Boston, radical welcome played out like this: the Monday Lunch Program started thirty years ago as a traditional feeding program. Suburban churches sent teams of volunteers into the city, and together with Cathedral leaders they prepared and served meals to the city's homeless and hungry.

When the program needed a new director, they hired Chris, a gifted and committed volunteer and formerly homeless guest who had just gotten his first apartment. Chris had

radical welcome: embracing the gifts, power, and voice of new groups, so they shape the church's life, even as the church shapes them

no social work degree, but no one knew the program inside-and-out better than he did. No one had more positive relationships with the other city programs, cultivated from years as a guest and volunteer. Because of his unique gifts, he helped to create a powerful culture of welcome, empowerment, and transformation, one that changed the lives of physically hungry guests and spiritually hungry suburban volunteers.

Following the Episcopal Way, we could become a community of rich and poor, privileged and underprivileged, who come together to share resources and participate in God's mission. We could live as a church that listens, embraces, and partners with neighbors of every kind.

TRY THIS   Invite a group from your church or community to take a walk around the neighborhood where you live or worship. Invite each person to observe and take notes on the signs of wellness and signs of brokenness. Talk to people in the neighborhood and ask about their experiences living or working in the area. Where are they seeing goodness? Where are they wishing a church would partner with them?

After the walk, gather as a group and invite each person to share a reflection. Then decide together who else you need to meet with and listen to in order to figure out what God is calling you to do in order to share or experience healing in this place.

Chapter 12

Falling in Love with God Again

Episcopalians openly and proudly build our faith on reason. Visit a church and you are likely to hear comments like, "Our faith is a thinking faith" and "Here you don't have to leave your brain at the door." We welcome people to bring their questions and their doubts inside as part of their offering to God.

Reason has not only shaped the Episcopal Way; it is core to being Christian. Through reason, we have interpreted scripture as a guide for living our faith. We have used our minds to create poetry, music, and arts for worshiping God. We have formed organizations with sound structures and creeds. Over more than two thousand years of Christian history, reason has been a constant companion, inspiring and leading us to follow Jesus in an always-changing world.

That said, reason has a special role in the Episcopal Way. Anglicanism came to life during a great paradigm shift: not just the Reformation, but the Renaissance. While the Reformation was advancing independence from the Roman Catholic Church, the common people's access to the scriptures, and thoughtful approaches to faith, the Renaissance was asking previously unthinkable questions about the divine, the human being, and the world.

Consider this: About the same moment Thomas Cranmer was composing the first Prayer Book (1549), Copernicus was introducing Italy to the idea that the earth is round and circles the sun (1543). At the time, both efforts looked like an affront to faithful Christians and an overreach by human reason. In hindsight, we can see that each man used reason to give glory to God.

The Limits of Reason

It is possible to be so confident about reason and the human capacity to explain everything that we forget about a God who is quite beyond us. Eric was offering a workshop at an Episcopal seminary and introduced them to an experiential way of listening to scripture. They read the passage three times and shared reflections after each reading. The final round ended with the question: "What does God invite you to do, change, or be through this passage?"

At the end of the reflection, a student said he was truly moved, partly because he had so rarely explored scripture at this experiential level. "I really have a hard time with the way the Bible is taught here. I'm surprised I have any faith left now that we've analyzed the Bible to death." Scholarly analysis of scriptures is critical, but reason should not be so highly privileged that it eclipses the other pathways for reaching God.

Road Rule 15 Take a moment in any situation—at home, at work, in school—and ask yourself: "Where is God in this situation? What would Jesus do here? Do any of the 'saints' in my life have anything to say to this?"

The tradition of a reasonable faith devoid of miracles and irrational elements has long been part of the American and English religious landscape. Think of former President Thomas Jefferson, who once claimed the authors of the Gospels were "ignorant, unlettered men" who laid "a groundwork of vulgar ignorance, of things impossible, of superstitions, fanaticisms, and fabrications."[44] In 1804 he took it upon himself to craft The Jefferson Bible, a more credible version with miracles removed.

Faith without reason is empty and potentially dangerous. But faith that relies too exclusively on reason can be hollow and—because it is so dependent on human faculties—not especially faithful at all. Reason may be one of the pillars of contemporary American culture; we still need the dynamic of scripture and tradition to make sure we do not simply disappear into our own heads.

There Are Many Reasons

Reason has other limits, especially when one group's definition of reason and thoughtfulness trumps the rest. It is much too easy to assume my way of reasoning is universal—if a group doesn't think like I do, they must be less intelligent. In fact, they may have a different but just as effective way of thinking.

We see this subtle privileging of one group's thinking all the time. For instance, lots of Episcopal churches host meetings using *Robert's Rules of Order*. However, this highly structured, rational, and rule-based process rises from a particular culture's way of reasoning and making decisions. Many people—especially those of us from Asian, Latino, Native American, or Black cultures, or those of us reared in different economic environments—come with different ways of relating, deciding, and thinking. If the church does not account for these differences, certain groups land on the margins, shut out of contributing or leading unless they master the dominant process.

---

44. Steven Waldman, "Deism: Alive and Well in America," *The Wall Street Journal* (September 23, 2009). Available at http://online.wsj.com/news/articles/SB125365145301031757

In a multi-cultural nation and world like ours, this kind of narrow definition of reason can foster bullying and domination—two things the Reformation and Renaissance were born to counter.

To Be in the World, But Not of It

The Episcopal Way is often quite comfortable using the language and reason of the culture around us. We also understand that Christians have a parallel calling that provides balance to the extremes of reason: do not become so identified with the world that you forget what it means to be representatives of Jesus in the world. "If you belonged to the world," Jesus warned his disciples, "the world would love you as its own. Because you do not belong to the world, but I have chosen you out of the world—therefore the world hates you" (John 15:19).

Episcopalians have a gift for embracing and living fully embedded in the world, and yet we are attempting to live a distinct life, a way shaped by the life of Jesus. With this balanced posture, we can use our reason, then pause and listen for God's voice and imagine how the compassion of God would make very different sense of a situation.

Sometimes, Episcopalians have gotten into trouble with existing power-holders precisely because they occupied this in-between state. Take a look at Jonathan Daniels, an Episcopal theological student in Massachusetts during the Civil Rights movement. The world told him what was sensible, especially for a young, privileged, white man. Instead, he left his spot in seminary, took a bus to Alabama, and gave his life as a martyr for the movement.

Take a look at our Anglican brother Archbishop Desmond Tutu. As a black South African, he experienced great humiliation under apartheid, but as an Anglican bishop he could have taken cover and ridden out the storm. Instead, he endangered his own life and the lives of his family members by opposing the Apartheid regime.

These men lived in the world but not of the world, stirred by something stronger than (and maybe even opposed to) reason. The Episcopal Way pulls us beyond the relative simplicity and comfort of reason, into the complexity of faith. How much simpler life would be, if we just acted reasonable and said little about our faith. Put down the Bible, because you might look like a "bible thumper." Do not clap, because you will look out of control. Participate in outreach and mission trips, but don't shove faith down anyone's throat.

But saints like Jonathan Daniels, Desmond Tutu, and so many more did not leave a mark because they were reasonable Christians. They were steeped in the Bible, unapologetic about their faith, and convinced they had a place in the ongoing story of God. And so do we.

Where is redemption for a church that is tempted to think itself out of relationship with God? What does a changing world need from the Episcopal Church? We feel certain they need us to follow Jesus' advice: love the Lord your God with all your heart, soul, strength, and mind; and love your neighbor as yourself (Luke 10:27).

In other words, follow the Episcopal Way. Bring together all the parts of who you are—brain, heart, flesh, spirit—and dedicate them all to loving God completely. There is no need to leave anything outside, not reason, not the scriptures, not your traditions, not your experiences. The most powerful, beautiful witness we could make is the one that unites all that we are and all that we have, as we walk the Way with the God we love.

TRY THIS Go to an Episcopal lectionary website (http://www .lectionarypage.net or another). You will notice that certain days have the name of a person or group on them: these are the people or groups we have identified as our "saints." Click on one of these names, and then search the Internet and read about their life and work. See if you feel inspired to deepen your own commitment and love for God.

Walking the Episcopal Way

Have you ever seen a dancer or figure skater launch into a gorgeous series of spins? Have you ever wondered how they could do all that turning and then ease out of it with no sign of dizziness? Dancers do something called "spotting": they identify a point, and with each revolution their eye returns to that spot. Everything around them may be turning—they may be spinning—but as long as they keep watching that still point, they will be balanced, strong, and beautiful.

Episcopalians know how to spot. We are deeply rooted in ancient traditions and structures—the Bible, the Eucharist, ordered worship, the ministry of our bishops, priests, deacons, and laypeople, historic statements of faith, and more. The world may spin—and God knows as a church we may spin—but as long as we don't forget how to spot, we will not fall down in a dizzy heap.

Given all the paradigm shifts we have described in this book, and the many other issues we have not even raised—changes in how we understand gender identity, sexuality, racial and ethnic identity, widening gaps between the rich and poor and the disappearance of an American middle class, the rising sense of insecurity since 9/11, and the rapid degradation of the environment—there is no doubt that America needs civil and religious institutions that can provide some centeredness to balance the chaos. We need to be confident, to love our roots, to share that love with the communities around us. If we do not remain grounded and love the story we carry, who will?

But what is that story? In other words, how do you know you are walking the Episcopal Way?

- The Episcopal Way travels the **Via Media,** a balanced "both/and" path that holds complexity and seeming contradiction without losing its hold on faith and truth.
- The Episcopal Way is **catholic and Protestant**, grounded in ancient sacrament and ordered prayer, yet willing to change to meet a changing world.
- The Episcopal Way rests on the **three-legged stool** of Scripture, Tradition, and Reason, all of which Christians must heed if we're going to follow Jesus and live as extensions of his body in the world.
- The Episcopal Way is deeply **incarnational** and follows the God who loved creation enough to dwell among us in flesh and blood.
- The Episcopal Way is **liturgical,** following ancient structures and common forms for worship even as we adapt to share the story of God in emerging cultures.
- The Episcopal Way is **networked,** locally and globally, and draws us into a web of relationship with a rich past, a broad present, and an unknown future.
- The Episcopal Way is **democratic,** valuing every baptized person as a minister of God, and setting out structures and ordered ministries in order to facilitate our participation in God's mission.
- The Episcopal Way celebrates the **Vernacular Principle** by translating the gospel and traditions into the language and culture of people on the ground.

The Episcopal Way is a way of **reason** and **mystery,** trusting there is a time to use our God-given reason and a time to rest in awe and wonder.

The Episcopal Way is flexible and **adaptive,** no longer bound by the fear of change.

The Episcopal Way lifts up **beauty,** because it offers a taste of heaven and stirs us to go seek and serve the Christ who shines beautifully in all people.

The Episcopal Way is **generous,** embracing people of all backgrounds and inviting each of us to contribute for the sake of God's kingdom.

The Episcopal Way is **in love with God,** the God we meet in Scripture, Tradition, and Reason, in flesh, nature, poetry, and art; in the whole creation that God has made and redeemed.

There is plenty to love, celebrate, and share about this generous, beautiful, incarnational, ancient and future way. But remember: it is a way. It is a path for walking, an approach to following Jesus, not just a set of prescriptions defining right belief and correct behavior. Can it change? Not only can it, but it must, if it is going to still be Anglican. Change is necessary, to meet new cultural contexts. Change is good, when it translates the gospel for new communities to hear, share, and follow Jesus Christ with their whole hearts. And change is holy, when we engage it faithfully and without losing our essence.

That is why we think it is so vital to get clear on the core elements of Anglican and Episcopal identity. When you see them spelled out, you realize they are distinct: the three-legged stool of Scripture, Tradition, and Reason; the Via Media; the incarnation; beauty and justice. They are also strong: Not one of these elements is compromised when it meets other cultures and languages. Not one loses its power in translation.

Take It Outside

Ultimately, it is not enough to understand the Episcopal Way. If there is one thing we know about being Episcopalian, it is that you have to practice it. And if there is one thing we know about the world today, it is that you cannot wait for someone to enter your church to find out what a great Christian you are. Walking the Episcopal Way has to take you outside.

From the opening acts of this book to these final pages, we have attempted to provide the content and practical tools that people need to take our faith and traditions outside. When someone asks, "What's the big deal about this Episcopal Church?" we think there is much to share, and it goes deeper than, "The beautiful liturgy" or "We're inclusive." And if there is not time to talk it out, we hope you might hand this book to a friend, colleague, student, or even to the person reading over your shoulder on the train.

Sharing the Christian story or your own may sound a bit scary. The good news is, you have genuinely good news to share. There are gifts in this Way that speak to a changing world full of contradictions and possibilities.

Our neighbors cry out for community and relationship, even as everyone wants to discover their individual voice and expression. So come to the Eucharist, where we all get knit into one body, the body of Jesus, and discover that we are beloved by God, just as we are. Technology makes it possible to connect in ways that sounded like the stuff of science fiction a decade ago, but all that over-sharing can leave us feeling overwhelmed and isolated. So read the scriptures in a group, and discover how your story fits into the story God has been unfolding through all of history.

If you love it, then understand it and share it. As long as the essence holds, be generous on the rest. If anything, we are convinced that the act of sharing and adapting our traditions for a changing world can make the gifts of the Episcopal Way sparkle even brighter. Have you ever heard an eighteenth-century hymn set to bass and percussion? Ever seen clergy vestments made of African kente cloth? Ever heard the evocative language of the New Zealand prayer book? That moment of surprise and even discomfort can be a moment for the Holy Spirit to come in and clarify a truth you never knew.

The Episcopal Way assumes God is still revealing truth and opening our hearts. What a blessing that Episcopal redemption rests in returning to the truth at the heart of our tradition. Few things are more faithful to the Episcopal Way than embodying the gospel in close relationship with the local contexts and cultures around us. May God bless you in your listening and in your walking.